edited by M J Breheny · London  n publication

developments in urban and regional analysis

KV-577-879

Pion Limited, 207 Brondesbury Park, London NW2 5JN

Copyright © 1979 by Pion Limited

All rights reserved. No part of this book may be produced in any form by photostat microfilm or any other means without written permission from the publishers.

ISBN 0 85086 078 4

Printed in Great Britain by Page Bros (Norwich) Limited

Contributors

D Booth   *Centre for Environmental Studies, 62 Chandos Place, London WC2N 4HH*

M Clarke   *School of Geography, University of Leeds, Leeds LS2 9JT*

J D Coelho   *Faculty of Science, University of Lisbon, Lisbon 2*

M G Coombes   *Department of Geography, University of Newcastle upon Tyne, Newcastle upon Tyne NE1 7RU*

J S Dixon   *Department of Geography, University of Newcastle upon Tyne, Newcastle upon Tyne NE1 7RU*

D Gleave   *Centre for Environmental Studies, 62 Chandos Place, London WC2N 4HH*

J B Goddard   *Department of Geography, University of Newcastle upon Tyne, Newcastle upon Tyne NE1 7RU*

S R Hashim   *Maharaja Sayajirao University of Baroda, Baroda 2, Gujarat*

G Hyman   *Centre for Environmental Studies, 62 Chandos Place, London WC2N 4HH*

J B Kau   *Department of Real Estate and Legal Studies, The University of Georgia, Athens, Georgia 30602*

C-F Lee   *Department of Economics, University of Illinois at Urbana-Champaign, Illinois 61801*

G Leonardi   *Faculty of Architecture, Polytechnic of Turin, Turin*

P N Mathur   *Department of Economics, University College of Wales, Aberystwyth SY23 3DB*

S Openshaw   *Department of Town and Country Planning, University of Newcastle upon Tyne, Newcastle upon Tyne NE1 7RU*

D Palmer   *Centre for Environmental Studies, 62 Chandos Place, London WC2N 4HH*

C F Sirmans   *Department of Real Estate and Legal Studies, The University of Georgia, Athens, Georgia 30602*

M W Smart   *28 The Lane, Blackheath, London SE3*

P J Taylor   *Department of Geography, University of Newcastle upon Tyne, Newcastle upon Tyne, NE1 7RU*

P M Townroe   *School of Economic and Social Studies, University of East Anglia, Norwich NR4 7TJ*

A G Wilson   *School of Geography, University of Leeds, Leeds LS2 9JT*

Contents

Introduction

M J BREHENY
Gloucestershire County Planning Department

This volume, the tenth in the *London Papers* series, presents a selection of papers from the annual conference of the British Section of the Regional Science Association held at University College London in September, 1978. The papers presented to the annual conference have never been restricted to a particular theme, the aim being to allow the conference to reflect the variety of work being carried out under the regional science umbrella. The conference has traditionally seen contributions from a wide variety of disciplines subjected to scrutiny by participants from different backgrounds and interests. The papers contained in this volume are presented in two groups, which together give an insight into some of the current preoccupations of regional scientists. The first group reflects the continuing concern with abstract theoretical issues, largely concerned with spatial analysis, that have been a feature of regional science for some time. The second group of papers is concerned in different ways with the analysis of industrial and employment issues in Britain, reflecting a contemporary concern of regional scientists with the policy issues that predominate in central and local government. The two groups of papers thus reflect a noticeable feature of regional science, namely the distinction between a core of ongoing, theoretical and abstract work, largely concerned with spatial and economic analysis, and more practical or empirical studies that are developed in response to contemporary policy issues or conceptual shifts.

In part 1 of this volume, the papers by Leonardi, Coelho, and Wilson and Clarke are all concerned with theoretical aspects of spatial analysis, but they also have a common concern with the synthesis of areas of understanding. Since Isard's idea of 'channels of synthesis' (Isard, 1960), a major feature of regional science has been the effort to link together independently initiated theoretical developments. This has been particularly noticeable in the fusing of ideas on gravity modelling and optimisation procedures. The papers by Leonardi and Coelho have a common root in the work carried out in this area. Leonardi aims to "provide a unified theoretical and operational approach to the problems of optimising the location of a set of spatially interacting variables". He starts by explaining how apparently different kinds of spatial interaction problem, such as the Lowry-type model and a health-care facility location model, have a common basic mathematical form. Given this, he proceeds to demonstrate how the mathematical programming model that he advocates can be applied to this class of problems. Coelho presents a locational-surplus maximisation model for land-use planning, and demonstrates how the model brings together work on linear optimisation

methods and the gravity or spatial interaction model. The use of the
maximisation model in assessing land-use plans for the town of Santo
André in Portugal is explained.

The paper by Wilson and Clarke attempts a synthesis of ideas imported
from the field of catastrophe theory, which has to date been subjected to
few empirical experiments in the social sciences, with the gravity model,
as applied in assessing urban retail structures. Results are presented in
which the 'jump' behaviour of catastrophe theory occurs in the modelling
of retail trip patterns in Leeds. The authors speculate about the potential
value of catastrophe theory in assessing the dynamics of urban change,
and ultimately in aiding policy formulation.

Kau, Lee, and Sirmans develop in their paper a well-established area of
research in regional science, which is concerned with the relationship
between distance and the density of development in urban areas. They
demonstrate the use of a variable elasticity of substitution (VES)
production function in deriving an urban land-use model to investigate the
impact of changing elasticity of substitution of land for capital on urban
structure. The value of this model is compared to alternatives which use
Cobb–Douglas or constant elasticity of substitution (CES) production
functions.

Whilst it is fundamentally a theoretical contribution, the paper by
Mathur stands in contrast to the others in this volume in that he is
concerned with economic developments at the world level, and in
particular with the relative trading positions of developed and developing
countries. He notes the continued dominance of the developed nations
in the world trade of manufactured goods, and attempts to quantify the
potential gains to be made by the developing countries if they develop
some form of 'collective self-reliance'. Given an observed inverse
relationship between per capita imports and population level, explained by
greater competition and production efficiency in countries with large
populations, Mathur uses this relationship to calculate the decrease in
imports that would result from the development of 'common markets'
amongst developing countries. Results are presented for the gains to be
made for differing levels of cooperation.

In part 2 of this volume, the paper by Palmer and Gleave aims to
develop a fuller understanding of the nature of the matchmaking process
between unemployed workers and vacant jobs; a process which has
become increasingly complex in highly specialised societies. The paper
begins with a review of the theoretical aspects of the process, and goes on
to develop a series of hypotheses concerning the relationship between job
mobility and the size of firm and the nature of quits and hirings. These
are then assessed with a series of empirical investigations on data for the
United Kingdom in the nineteen-seventies.

The contributions by Booth and Hyman and by Townroe, whilst dealing
with issues that have a bearing on current policy concerns, develop areas

of work that have been familiar to regional scientists for some time. Booth and Hyman present an exploratory analysis of the nature of population and employment change in urban areas. They estimate predictive models, using time-series data, for Walsall in the West Midlands of England, in which the relationship between industrial sectors, and particularly between supposedly basic and nonbasic industries, is assessed. They draw conclusions on both the major determinants of change in the study area and certain methodological issues.

In his paper, Townroe tries to identify the impact of different aspects of agglomeration economies on the performance of individual industrial sectors, as measured by output per head, and thus on regional economic growth. Following a review of related work, the paper presents the results of regression analyses on the relationship between industrial performance and a set of agglomeration variables. The inconclusive results imply either that the methodology adopted and the variables used were inappropriate, or that such agglomeration economies are, indeed, not important.

The paper by Coombes et al reflects the recent interest in Britain in defining appropriate geographical areas for the analysis of industrial and employment issues. The paper reviews the problems of producing such regionalisations and evaluates one recent major attempt in the United Kingdom. An alternative regionalisation is presented with, it is claimed, a better conceptual and empirical base. In his comment on the Coombes et al paper, Smart questions the overriding concern in such work with definitions based on the notion of centrality, and argues for practical regionalisations 'grounded in experience'.

The 1978 annual conference of the British section of the Regional Science Association marked a decade of such events, and provides the opportunity for a brief reflection on the changes in content and orientation of the papers presented over this period. The dozen or so papers contained in each volume of *London Papers* provide a very small sample from which to judge the contemporary preoccupations of regional scientists. Nevertheless, the sequence of ten volumes gives a surprisingly comprehensive picture of changes that have occurred, albeit one drawn from a largely British perspective.

A hard core of regional science work has persisted throughout the period, focussing on spatial analysis and location theory, although the approaches have been developing and shifting. Other areas of work have reflected more closely changing fashions and priorities, changes which have often occurred not just in regional science but in the social sciences more generally. In the late sixties and early seventies the common denominator to regional science, in common with other social sciences, appeared to be mathematical analysis, as reflected in the early volumes of *London Papers*. Because much of the mathematical modelling work was concerned with the ultimate practical value of the models, the use of regional science methods in land-use planning became a regular feature of conferences, and has remained a strong theme in British regional science.

Since the early seventies, the contributions to the conference, and hence to *London Papers*, have become increasingly diverse, reflecting the aim of allowing the conference both to reflect and stimulate the changing and expanding nature of the field. Papers concerned with philosophical, political, and ideological aspects of regional science have supplemented, and in many cases challenged, the established core of research work. This diversity is more pronounced in Britain than in, say, the United States, where regional science is supposedly much stronger, because of the desire of the British Section of the Association to add empirical and practical work to the standard theoretical diet, and continually to inject new ideas and invite different perspectives into the debate. It is because of this approach that, despite its apparently modest nature, the annual conference of the British Section of the Regional Science Association, and the associated *London Papers* series, have been consistently an important focus for interdisciplinary study.

Reference
Isard W, 1960 *Methods of Regional Analysis* (MIT Press, Cambridge, Mass)

Some Illustrations of Catastrophe Theory Applied to Urban Retailing Structures

A G WILSON, M CLARKE
University of Leeds

1 Introduction

The increasing interest in and growing application of catastrophe theory in the social sciences has been marked by the lack of empirical evidence to supplement the qualitative detail (see, for example, Poston and Stewart, 1978). Indeed it is to some extent the lack of empirical experimentation that has raised doubts as to the efficacy of using catastrophe theory as a tool of investigation in the social sciences (Zahler and Sussman, 1977).

In this paper we explicitly focus on an attempt to translate theory into practice. The area of concern is the dynamics of urban retailing structure, and to this end we expand on a recent paper by Harris and Wilson (1978). The difficulties of implementing numerical experiments to illustrate such theoretical work and the insights then generated are discussed, and some numerical results are presented.

It is argued that catastrophe theory can serve at least two useful purposes in the area of interest. First it offers new insights into the dynamics of the urban retailing structure, which have an economic interpretation. Second it could ultimately be used as an aid to planning, in predicting effects of certain policies, and as an aid to policy formulation.

2 Insights to be sought from catastrophe theory

Consider a model of the form

$$x = \mathbf{f}(y, u) , \tag{1}$$

where the components of the vector x are (dependent) state variables, those of y are to be taken as constants, and those of u as independent variables, often referred to as control variables. The inclusion of the vector y simply recognises that most models in practice will include 'constants' which can be largely ignored, though occasionally there will be a transfer of variables from y to u.

Relationship (1) defines a *manifold* (or surface) in (x, u) space. As the independent control variables, written $u(t)$ say, change over time, then so also does x, as $x(t)$, and the point $[x(t), u(t)]$ traces out a trajectory on the manifold. Dynamic analysis is concerned with the nature of such trajectories. Catastrophe theory is concerned with the special case of systems where relationship (1) is the result of a maximisation process, say of

$$\text{maximise} \, Z = Z(x, y, u) . \tag{2}$$
$$\quad x, u$$

The surface (1) is, typically, folded and this generates dynamic behaviour which is different from the usual smooth and reversible changes of equilibrium models. The effects involved are *jumps* (discrete change in a dependent variable caused by a very small change in an independent variable), *divergence* (the system taking alternative trajectories for very small differences in control-variable values), and *hysteresis* (the return to an original state after a disturbance, but taking a different path).

In this paper we will be mainly concerned with jumps. One of the main features of catastrophe theory is that it characterises in a general way the types of jump behaviour which are possible and establishes that, for any system governed by an equation like equation (2), the types of jump (locally, in state space) depend only on the number of control variables. For small numbers of u variables, this generates Thom's (1975) seven elementary catastrophes, and we will be concerned mainly with the most elementary of all, the fold catastrophe, which arises when there is a single control variable (which involves, temporarily, the assumption that other possible control variables are in y; that is, taking two-dimensional slices of higher-dimensional manifolds). The results of the theory are not dependent on the number of state variables. In theory, transformations are available to represent them in canonical form. These are difficult to handle in practice, however.

One of the main points to be taken from catastrophe theory is the need to be alert to the possibility of discrete change. This consciousness can be beneficial even when the detailed results of the theory cannot be applied. This is the spirit in which catastrophe theory is used in this paper: the results could be derived without the theory, but the awareness of the possibility of discrete change and the interpretation of the results in catastrophe-theory terms have helped considerably.

3 Urban retailing structures
3.1 The model to be used
The work reported here is based on the well-known Huff (1964) and Lakshmanan and Hansen (1965) shopping model

$$S_{ij} = A_i e_i P_i W_j^\alpha \exp(-\beta c_{ij}) , \qquad (3)$$

where

$$A_i = \left[\sum_j W_j^\alpha \exp(-\beta c_{ij}) \right]^{-1} , \qquad (4)$$

S_{ij} is the flow of sales from residences in zone i to shops in zone j;
e_i is per capita expenditure in zone i;
P_i is the population of zone i;
W_j is the size of the centre in zone j (and is taken as a measure of
        attractiveness);
c_{ij} is the usual cost-matrix element; and
α and β are parameters.

3.2 Structural dynamics

The retailing structural variables in the model are the W_j. The usual use of the model is to calculate the S_{ij} for given (trial) W_j and hence to compute $\sum_i S_{ij}$ ($= D_j$, say), the turnover in zone j, from that overall allocation of centre sizes. It is possible though to add equations to the system which determine the W_j under some hypothesis. A number of ways of doing this are discussed in detail in Harris and Wilson (1978) and so they will only be sketched here. Fortunately, because of the highly constrained nature of the problem, all the approaches lead to the same predictions for the W_j.

The simplest hypothesis for the W_j is that producers of shopping centres 'balance' revenue and supply and that a relation of the following kind holds:

$$\sum_i S_{ij} = kW_j \, , \tag{5}$$

where k can be considered as a constant that measures sales generated per unit of floorspace. (In some circumstances it may be useful to have it varying by zone, as k_j, but this does not affect the essence of the theoretical argument and is not pursued here.) Equations (3), (4), and (5) can then be solved for the W_j and $W_j(t)$ calculated as a sequence if any of the independent variables change.

An equivalent mathematical programme to determine the W_j arises from a consumers'-surplus-maximisation problem (cf Coelho and Wilson, 1976):

$$\underset{S_{ij}, W_j}{\text{maximise}} \, Z = -\frac{1}{\beta} \sum_{i,j} S_{ij} \ln S_{ij} + \sum_{i,j} S_{ij} \left(\frac{\alpha}{\beta} \ln W_j - c_{ij} \right) \tag{6}$$

subject to

$$\sum_j S_{ij} = e_i P_i \tag{7}$$

and

$$\sum_j W_j = W \, , \tag{8}$$

where W is the total amount of 'size'—say floorspace—to be allocated. An alternative, and again equivalent, formulation due to Leonardi (1978) shows that k in equation (5) is proportional to (and, with suitable choice of units, equal to) the Lagrangian multiplier associated with equation (8) in the programming problem. Formulation (6)–(8) is the one we have used to obtain the W_j in the empirical work described later in this paper. We show later that this procedure does produce jumps in the W_j for small changes in parameter values.

This information can be recorded as on figure 3, and the $\alpha > 1$ case produces a diagram which is characteristic of the fold catastrophe.

A feature of the argument which generates figure 1 is that the form of the relationship between D_j and W_j for a particular j is deduced on an 'other terms remaining constant' basis. This will not usually be the case in practice, particularly as constraint (8) usually has to be satisfied. Thus one of the main purposes of this paper is to obtain curves of the form of figure 1 for numerical data and to check out the associated fold-catastrophe behaviour. The 'other terms remaining constant' assumption has caused considerable difficulties in practice and has made the interpretation of our numerical work far from easy. This has led both to new theoretical insights and to major new problems for research, and these are reported separately later.

There is a further complication: we might expect shopping-centre capacity to expand with available spending power. Equation (13) then suggests that k should remain roughly constant over time. If, as we argued earlier, the technology of supply improves, and k contains a factor which reflects this, then k may fall over time (and W increase more rapidly than $\sum_i e_i P_i$). Then, for some zones, k may decrease past k_j^{crit} and there could be a jump from $W_j = 0$ to $W_j = W_j^{\text{A}}$. This illustrates the nature of this theory as a contribution to geographical analysis: the modelling of the spatial evolution of structure which may involve discrete change of this type.

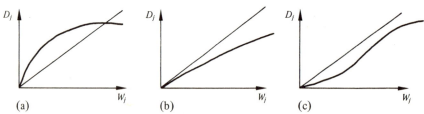

Figure 2. The disappearance of W_j^{A} for large k_j: (a) $\alpha < 1$; (b) $\alpha = 1$; (c) $\alpha > 1$.

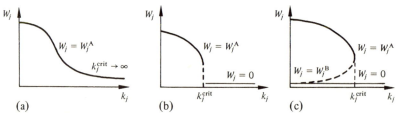

Figure 3. The equilibrium points as a function of k_j: (a) $\alpha < 1$; (b) $\alpha = 1$; (c) $\alpha > 1$.

3.3.2 Changes in β

The parameter β measures 'ease of travel' for the consumer: the higher the value of β the more difficult it is to travel. It has been shown elsewhere (Poston and Wilson, 1977) that for the model given by equations (3) and (4), the W_j are likely to change smoothly for changing β, and we have already commented that the pattern will change from a dispersed one to a centralised one as β changes from a high value to a low one. This could also be interpreted in terms of central-place theory as a change from a large number of low-order facilities to a situation with a dominant high-order structure. However, it was also shown in the same paper that if the attractiveness term, W_j^α, was topologically 'like' a logistic function, for example, if W_j^α was replaced by

$$V = \exp\left\{\frac{\gamma}{[1 + \gamma \exp(-\delta W_j)]}\right\}, \tag{16}$$

then as β decreases there is a critical value β_j^{crit} for zone j at which W_j can jump to a higher value. In this case the jump is likely to be from a small nonzero value to a higher one (or vice versa) as against the zero to nonzero transitions for changes in k.

Historically β has decreased over a long time period, and this analysis suggests (whether by smooth or discrete change) that this will have contributed to the development of a smaller number of larger centres—a less dispersed pattern. We should also note that this section can be considered, in a broad sense, to cover changes in the c_{ij}, though spatially differentiated changes will of course have spatial structural consequences.

3.3.3 Changes in α

The parameter α can be considered as a measure of consumers' scale economies: if $\alpha > 1$, for example, there are increasing returns to scale. There is no theoretical evidence yet that it causes discrete change, though it is apparent that it can cause second-order jumps or constraint catastrophe jumps as we will see shortly. Empirical evidence suggests that α is usually close to 1 (which is in a sense a critical value because it distinguishes the three cases in figure 1).

3.3.4 Second-order effects

The effects to be considered here are second-order in that we are concerned with the effect of changes in α and β on the position of k_j^{crit}, but the consequences may be major. As α or β change, the shapes of the curves in figure 1 change. Consider β as the simplest example. For low β, consumers will be more inclined to travel to larger centres; for high β, they will use local centres whatever the attractiveness of high W_j values elsewhere. The corresponding curves (for $\alpha > 1$) are sketched in figure 4. Thus, as β changes, the higher β, the higher k_j^{crit} will be, and hence the more probable it is that it will exceed k in a particular zone and hence produce $W_j \neq 0$ for that zone.

In effect the analysis for $\alpha \leqslant 1$ is contained in figure 1. For $\alpha > 1$, as α increases, centres with large W_j will become relatively more attractive and so the α behaviour is the mirror image of figure 4.

It is clear from this analysis that jumps are just as likely for small changes in α or β when these take values close to those which produce a revenue curve which touches $D_j = kW_j$. For given k and α, there will exist a β, say β_j^{crit}, for which the revenue curve and $D_j = kW_j$ touch. As α varies with k remaining fixed, β_j^{crit} will vary as sketched in figure 5. (Though we should emphasise that the exact shape of this curve has yet to be investigated.) Note that this argument could have been presented the other way round: for fixed k and given β, there exists an α, say α_j^{crit}, for which curve and line touch. This of course must generate the same curve as that shown in figure 5: in effect we are finding the set of points $(\alpha_j^{crit}, \beta_j^{crit})$ which produce the set of curves which touch $D_j = kW_j$, as shown in figure 6. This means that the horizontal axis of figure 5 can be labelled α_j^{crit}. Note that, as k then varies, the point $(k, \alpha_j^{crit}, \beta_j^{crit})$ traces out a surface.

We defined k_j^{crit} earlier (as a function of α and β). We can now see that if α and β (as exogenous parameters) are close to α_j^{crit} and β_j^{crit} for the particular k (as a given exogenous parameter), then this means that, for zone j, $k_j^{crit} = k$, and therefore a small change in any of k, α, or β could produce jumps. Information on this would be of considerable importance to planners.

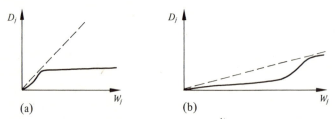

Figure 4. Revenue curves for (a) β high, k_j^{crit} high; and (b) β low, k_j^{crit} low.

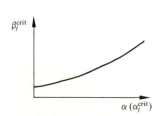

Figure 5. A plot of α (and in fact α_j^{crit}) versus β_j^{crit} for fixed k.

Figure 6. The set of curves which touch $D_j = kW_j$.

4 Some theoretical extensions arising from numerical experiments

4.1 Introduction

A common feature of numerical experimentation is that it exposes difficulties in the theory as previously stated and leads to extensions of the theory and to the formulation of new research problems. This has been very much the case here, and we deliberately present our thoughts in this form rather than as a body of post-hoc-integrated theory.

4.2 The revenue curve and the W_l, $l \neq j$, pattern

We noted earlier that the revenue curve, which is presently at the foundation of our analysis of possible jumps, depends on 'other terms remaining constant'. In practice this is simply not possible in any literal sense, and for numerical experiments it is necessary to make an explicit assumption about this. It turns out that the assumptions each have varying degrees of unsatisfactoriness. Four possibilities are discussed in turn here. We use the subscript j to denote the zone we are focusing attention on, the other zones are denoted by the subscript l.

Assumption 1: This is essentially the Harris and Wilson (1978) assumption: that other terms *do* remain constant while (for a focus on a particular zone j) W_j changes. This can be expressed as

$$W_j = \mu W^{\text{init}}, \qquad 0 \leqslant \mu < \infty, \tag{17}$$

and

$$W_l = W_l^{\text{init}}, \qquad l \neq j, \tag{18}$$

where μ is a parameter which ranges from 0 to a suitably large number, W^{init} is the initial value of W, and the W_l^{init} are the initial (and therefore in some sense 'realistic') values of the W_l, $l \neq j$. The main problem here is that the value of k changes. Equation (13), which is repeated here for convenience, gave

$$k = \sum_i \frac{e_i P_i}{W}. \tag{19}$$

Because W_j changes, while all the other W_l remain fixed, as μ varies, so does W as

$$W = \sum_{l \neq j} W_l^{\text{init}} + \mu W^{\text{init}}. \tag{20}$$

It can easily be seen that k decreases as μ increases, and so the $D_j = kW_j$ line should now be written as

$$D_j = k(W_j)W_j \tag{21}$$

(showing k as a function of W_j) with

$$k(W_j) = \left(\sum_i e_i P_i \right) \bigg/ \left(\sum_{l \neq j} W_l^{\text{init}} + W_j \right). \tag{22}$$

This creates graphs such as those shown in figure 7, for an $\alpha > 1$ case, and so should not in principle affect the general argument. The three possible cases of intersection, tangency, and nonintersection are also shown.

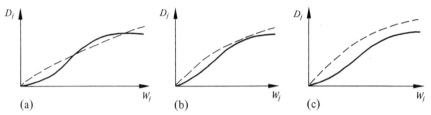

(a)   (b)   (c)

Figure 7. Three possible revenue curves for $\alpha > 1$, showing (a) intersection, (b) tangency, and (c) nonintersection.

Assumption 2: An obvious alternative is to make an assumption in which W is fixed. This involves deciding how the W_l, $l \neq j$, should decrease as W_j increases. A proportionate decrease is specified as

$$W_j = \mu W, \qquad 0 \leqslant \mu \leqslant 1, \tag{23}$$

and

$$W_l = W_l^{\text{init}}(1 - \mu), \qquad l \neq j; \tag{24}$$

then

$$\sum_l W_l = \sum_{l \neq j} W_l + W_j = W \tag{25}$$

for a constant W. Equation (13) still gives k, which remains constant for changing μ.

The problem with this assumption is that as μ approaches 1, $W_l \to 0$, for $l \neq j$, and, because there is therefore no competition for zone j, D_j simply increases unrealistically to kW as indicated in figure 8. This means that the results are only meaningful for much smaller values of μ—and these have to be investigated experimentally.

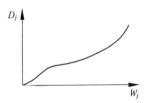

Figure 8. The revenue curve for assumption 2.

4.3 The interpretation of jumps

One obvious aim in the numerical experiments is to produce plots of the form of figure 1 (or figure 7) in relation to which we can identify critical values of the parameters (k, α, β) and then to relate these to a corresponding W_j jump produced by the mathematical programme (6)–(8). In this way we can 'interpret' such jumps in relation to an underlying mechanism and feel some confidence in our procedure for identifying critical regions (in fact, a surface, as we argued) of the (k, α, β) parameter space. This has led to our more serious theoretical problem as revealed by the numerical experiments. Figures 9(a) and 9(b) show the critical cases relating to assumptions 1 and 2 respectively. For the critical points we can run the mathematical programme for the neighbourhood of corresponding values of k, W, α, and β. However, the programme will then generate a set of W_l which do not correspond to the underlying W_l, $l \neq j$, pattern assumed in the construction of the curve.

The nature of this problem is different for the two assumptions. In the first case, if we locate a mathematical-programming (MP) W_j jump, there are two sets of 'corresponding' W_ls, $l \neq j$—those before and after the jump, say $\{W_l^{(1)}\}$ and $\{W_l^{(2)}\}$ respectively. It is then possible to construct figure 1/figure 7 plots by use of, in turn, $W_l^{init} = W_l^{(1)}$ and $W_l^{init} = W_l^{(2)}$ in the hope that this produces critical graphs approached from each side of the jump. The problem is that the W at which criticality occurs on the graph may be slightly different from the W (and k) assumed for the mathematical programme, and the MP solution may then be different for *that* W. This suggested procedure will be referred to as assumption $1'$.

For assumption 2 the problem is simpler: W_l, $l \neq j$, is constructed from equation (24) and there is no reason why this should ever correspond to a set of MP W_ls.

These difficulties lead us to formulate a third assumption.

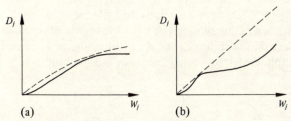

Figure 9. Criticality: (a) assumption 1; (b) assumption 2.

Assumption 3: This involves producing a revenue curve, for given k, W, α, and β, by adding a constraint

$$W_j = \mu W \tag{26}$$

to mathematical programme (6)–(8). This in effect fixes W_j and produces a set of W_ls which corresponds to the MP solution. This of course is a very different kind of W_l, $l \neq j$, background pattern for W_j variation: it is neither constant as in assumption 1 nor smoothly varying as in assumption 2. This in effect is the reverse of assumption $1'$.

Assumption 4: The final step in the argument involves a speculation about reality! The underlying purpose of the paper is to argue the possibility that spatial structure may evolve in a way which, in part, involves jumps. Say zone j is one such zone. Then, as W_j passes through a jump, the W_l, $l \neq j$, pattern will have changed in some (let us assume, monitored) way. The essence of the point here is that a W_j jump could occur in the neighbourhood of a set of existing W_ls, and that the revenue curve only has meaning in that neighbourhood. Thus perhaps there is a case for focusing not on the whole revenue curve but on small parts of it, each near a pattern which has occurred (or can occur?) in reality. This may imply, in effect, the use of something like assumption 3 for a region of W_j near to some existing W_l, $l \neq j$, pattern.

4.4 The revenue curve and the $e_i P_i$ pattern
We have assumed that our numerical experiments to date should largely be constructed for a given and fixed $e_i P_i$ pattern. However, three qualifying points should be noted about this and will be explored in a later paper. First there is the possibility of some W_j jumps taking place as a function of $e_i P_i$ changes, and these should be explored. Second this is particularly important since the changing W_j pattern in a city over a long period of time will certainly be determined as much by $e_i P_i$ changes (such as increasing incomes, social polarisation, or suburbanisation) as by changes in k, W, α, or β. Third a particular $e_i P_i$ pattern may affect, for particular zones, the shape of the revenue curves outlined in figure 1 and throughout the paper. We give one example of this. Consider a zone j for which $e_j P_j$ is small, and a situation in which β is relatively large. Then for low and increasing W_j, D_j will pick up rapidly to $e_j P_j / k$. Then, because of the high β, there may be relatively little increase. But for W_j beyond a certain point, D_j may increase with trips from other zones and this could lead to a double inflexion as sketched in figure 10, and this will lead to more complicated jump behaviour than outlined hitherto.

Figure 10. Possible double inflexion for low $e_j P_j$.

5 Experimental method

5.1 Computational procedures

To solve equations (6)–(8) or equation (9) we employed the same
computer program, but modified from a planning mode, which Coelho
and Wilson (1976) used for the problem of optimally locating the *total*
retail floorspace, W. The primal problem [equations (6)–(8)] is a nonlinear
programming problem with linear constraints, the dual [equation (9)] an
unconstrained nonlinear minimisation problem. The programming package
we used is based on a reduced-gradient method developed by Guigou
(1975).

The computing time required to achieve an optimal solution depends
largely on the number of variables in the problem. With eight zones, and
hence sixty-four S_{ij} terms, there are seventy-two variables, and typically
this may require 200–300 seconds of CPU time on the University of Leeds
ICL 1906A. Because of the large number of such runs involved in this
type of work, we chose to concentrate the programming efforts at the
University of Manchester Regional Computing Centre, where run time
could be reduced to about 20 seconds on their CDC 7600. Alternatively
the use of the dual formulation with a much reduced number of variables
(seventeen) for the same problem could be employed, but at the expense
of the S_{ij} terms, though these can easily be calculated. The run time is
usually also reduced by the input of starting values for the variables that
are close to the solution.

5.2 Data

As we were restricted by the limits of the mathematical-programming
algorithm, we used data for the Leeds City Region divided into only eight
zones (see figure 11). The data used are aggregates of Leeds ward data
from the 1966 Census, supplemented by data obtained in a small survey
carried out by students. Thus the numbers used are broadly realistic, but
are only used to illustrate the theoretical argument and how we now have
an empirically well-defined problem which could be tackled when better

Figure 11. The Leeds study area.

data become available. Exogenous inputs to the model are the cost matrix, $[c_{ij}]$, the expenditure and population pattern, given by the vector $[e_i P_i]$, the total floorspace, W, and the parameters α and β. These (except for W, α, and β) are given in table 1. The model outputs are strongly dependent on these exogenous inputs and, without dwelling too long on this point here, it is worth noting that our data are very crude and the zoning system we use (see figure 11) unsatisfactory. This does not necessarily affect our exploratory theoretical analysis, but it may produce misleading patterns of the W_j in comparison with the real world. Typically, however, we would not expect a pattern of optimum locations even from a more refined data set to match up with on-the-ground patterns for a variety of reasons.

Table 1. Data inputs $[e_i P_i]$ and $[c_{ij}]$.

$$[e_i P_i] = \begin{bmatrix} 18\,138 & 271\,825 & 270\,822 & 165\,258 & 154\,248 & 409\,652 & 478\,251 & 214\,547 \end{bmatrix}$$

$$[c_{ij}] = \begin{bmatrix}
11\cdot63 & 12\cdot10 & 12\cdot65 & 12\cdot89 & 11\cdot84 & 15\cdot29 & 15\cdot81 & 14\cdot91 \\
18\cdot09 & 14\cdot31 & 17\cdot91 & 19\cdot81 & 20\cdot13 & 16\cdot86 & 18\cdot44 & 24\cdot04 \\
17\cdot66 & 19\cdot08 & 14\cdot43 & 16\cdot46 & 17\cdot45 & 21\cdot89 & 15\cdot94 & 17\cdot70 \\
19\cdot98 & 21\cdot28 & 17\cdot41 & 15\cdot87 & 20\cdot68 & 25\cdot48 & 19\cdot17 & 15\cdot81 \\
17\cdot68 & 18\cdot75 & 17\cdot85 & 19\cdot31 & 15\cdot90 & 17\cdot36 & 20\cdot73 & 21\cdot33 \\
19\cdot74 & 18\cdot18 & 21\cdot66 & 22\cdot94 & 17\cdot48 & 14\cdot62 & 22\cdot25 & 25\cdot22 \\
16\cdot68 & 17\cdot42 & 14\cdot50 & 18\cdot39 & 17\cdot26 & 19\cdot98 & 10\cdot88 & 15\cdot66 \\
20\cdot09 & 22\cdot39 & 18\cdot37 & 16\cdot68 & 20\cdot49 & 25\cdot09 & 16\cdot57 & 12\cdot97
\end{bmatrix}$$

6 Numerical results

6.1 W_j patterns as functions of α and β

Despite certain vagaries within our data set, the W_j patterns generated by different values of α and β confirm the results derived by, amongst others, Harris (private communication) and White (1977). That is, for low β the most accessible zone (suitably defined) gains large shares of the total floorspace, W; for high β the W_j configuration reflects closely the $e_i P_i$ pattern, as the effect of β forces more people to patronise local facilities.

Increasing the attractiveness factor, α, has a similar effect to reducing β: the tendency is for large centres to grow further and for small centres to decline. Combined changes in α and β hence either amplify the trend (say, increasing α, decreasing β) or nullify it (for example, increasing α, increasing β).

6.2 Some examples of mathematical-programming jumps

Here we present several examples of jumps we have discovered from runs of the mathematical programme involving smoothly changing one or more of the parameter values. We do not attempt to demonstrate precisely why these jumps occur at this stage as the analysis in section 4.2 showed that this proves particularly tricky, although we hope to be able to proceed further to this stage soon.

The first example [figure 12(a)] shows a jump occurring in zone 1 for a small change in β, with $\alpha = 1$. Figure 12(b) illustrates a W_j jump for changing k, derived by changing the total stock, W, with $\alpha = 1 \cdot 3$, $\beta = 0 \cdot 5$. This resembles the fold catastrophe (for $\alpha > 1$, shown in figure 1). There is also the possibility of jumps occurring when more than one parameter is changing. It is probably the case generally that as several parameters

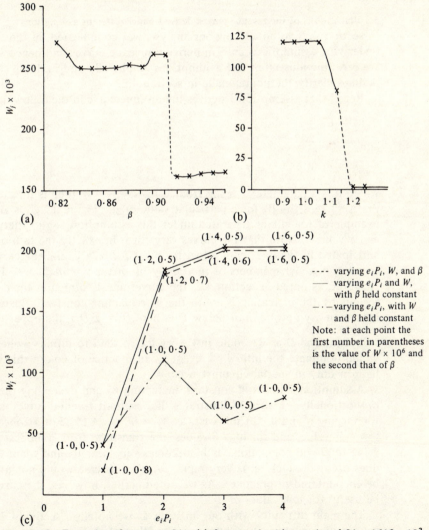

Figure 12. Examples of jumps in W_j: (a) for zone 1 with $\alpha = 1$ and $W = 1612 \times 10^3$, by varying β; (b) for zone 6 with $\alpha = 1 \cdot 3$ and $\beta = 0 \cdot 5$, by varying W and hence k; (c) for zone 2, by varying different combinations of $e_i P_i$, W, and β.

are changing only one is responsible for the jump, though double criticality may occur (see section 4.2). Figure 12(c) illustrates some W_j trajectories in the three-dimensional space of varying $e_i P_i$, W (and hence k), and β. Although it is too early to postulate that all these trajectories contain jumps of the type reported earlier, figure 12(c) does indicate the complex dynamics of our system of interest—we hope that further research will enable us to locate critical regions in the multidimensional parameter space within which jumps can be expected to occur along the lines of figure 5.

6.3 Illustrations of the revenue curves derived under different assumptions

In section 4.2 we noted how our analysis was complicated by the underlying assumptions used in deriving revenue curves and hence k_j^{crit}. We can now illustrate these assumptions empirically and in doing so perhaps clarify the points made in section 4.2.

Recall that assumption 1 derives the revenue curve in the following way:

$$W_j = \mu W^{\text{init}} \tag{27}$$

and

$$W_l = W_l^{\text{init}}, \qquad l \neq j, \tag{28}$$

where μ is a parameter ranging from 0 to, say, 1. W then is the sum of the W_l^{init} plus the W_j for a particular value of μ. Figure 13 gives an example of the curves generated under this assumption for a variety of α and β values. Note that the curves vary for α in exactly the fashion as anticipated in figure 1, with a logistic curve for $\alpha > 1$, and the curves for $\alpha = 1$ and $\alpha < 1$ members of the family of curves $y = mx^n$, $n \leq 1$. However, as noted in section 4.2, the curves are deformed in their upper regions by the increasing W_j, with the W_l remaining constant. Instead of having an asymptotic limit below D (where $D = \sum_j D_j$), the upper limit will always be D as we could in theory let W_j tend to infinity, where it would dominate the inflow of revenue. In practice of course this would happen only in special circumstances.

Assumption 2 holds W constant, increasing W_j and decreasing the W_l proportionally. Figure 14 illustrates the resultant revenue curves, again for varying α and β. In this case, as $W_j \to W$, $D_j \to D$. For a zone with a low $e_i P_i$ value, and for high β values, the transition from a modest D_j value to D will come along as W_j becomes very near W, and when this does occur the pick up is very rapid. Again this case would not usually be encountered in practice. As we noted earlier, however, the curves may be useful for low values of μ.

The main difficulty with our analysis, as we noted in section 4.2, is that we can construct revenue curves under either of these two assumptions, plot $D_j = kW_j$, and locate potential k_j^{crit} points for a given W_j, α, β combination. However, when we input these values into the mathematical

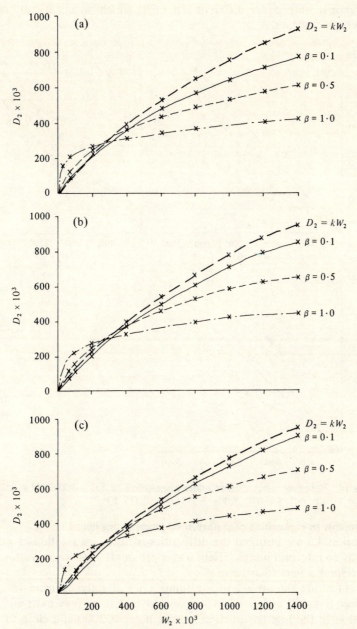

Figure 13. Revenue curves derived under assumption 1, for zone 2 with $W = 1 \cdot 7 \times 10^6$:
(a) $\alpha = 0 \cdot 9$; (b) $\alpha = 1 \cdot 0$; (c) $\alpha = 1 \cdot 1$.

programme, we produce different sets of W_l which do not usually relate to these k_j^{crit} values.

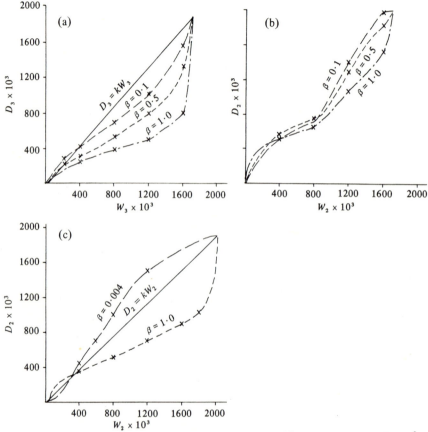

Figure 14. Revenue curves derived under assumption 2: (a) $\alpha = 0 \cdot 7$, $W = 1 \cdot 7 \times 10^6$; (b) $\alpha = 1 \cdot 0$, $W = 1 \cdot 7 \times 10^6$; (c) $\alpha = 1 \cdot 3$, $W = 2 \cdot 0 \times 10^6$.

6.4 Towards an explanation of mathematical-programming jumps
In section 4.3 we outlined the difficulties of using assumptions 1 and 2 directly to interpret jumps. Here we report an attempt to use assumption 1′ to interpret a particular jump.

We illustrate the problem for assumption 1 directly in figure 15. Between $\beta = 0 \cdot 2$ and $\beta = 0 \cdot 3$ it appeared that there may exist an inflexion in the logistic function around $W_j = 400000$ and close to the $D_j = kW_j$ curve. Therefore we ran the mathematical programme for a range of β values around this point, with $W = \sum_{l \neq j} W_l^{init} + W_j = 2 \cdot 1 \times 10^6$.

The set of W_ls that produced the logistic function, for $W = 2 \cdot 1 \times 10^6$, and the corresponding set of W_ls from the mathematical programme, for

$\beta = 0 \cdot 2$, are given in table 2. Clearly there is quite a dissimilarity between some W_ls; and although the overall pattern is similar this difference makes comparison infeasible. We therefore can make little use of assumption 1 directly to locate k_j^{crit} points on the revenue curves, with a corresponding transfer of the analysis to the mathematical programme and jump behaviour. We also face the problem of not being able to draw the revenue curves from the mathematical programme at the area of jumps because, by definition, the curves are broken around this point.

These empirical observations imply that we still have to locate jumps and then to try and explain why they occur. This is unsatisfactory both from a theoretical and from an empirical viewpoint. It obviously

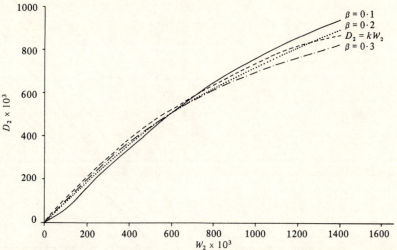

Figure 15. Revenue curves derived under assumption 1, for zone 2 with $\alpha = 1 \cdot 2$ and $\sum_{l \neq 2} W_l^{init} = 1\,700\,000$.

Table 2. The W_j values producing the revenue curve and those derived from the mathematical programme.

Zone	W_j	
	revenue curve	mathematical programme
1	62622	81097
2	400000	191016
3	330121	330465
4	69518	397460
5	9957	12458
6	121075	122510
7	868721	856663
8	237986	108327
W	$2 \cdot 10 \times 10^6$	$2 \cdot 10 \times 10^6$

necessitates considerably more intensive searching of the parameter space, and thus requires extra computing resources. In addition when jumps are found it is often difficult to link what is happening in practice with what *should* be happening in theory. Clearly this problem demands further research.

Once we have located a jump there does exist one approximation technique, referred to in section 4.3 as assumption 1′, which allows us to gain some possible insights into what is happening. If, for a point just before a jump, we can obtain the set of W_is from the mathematical

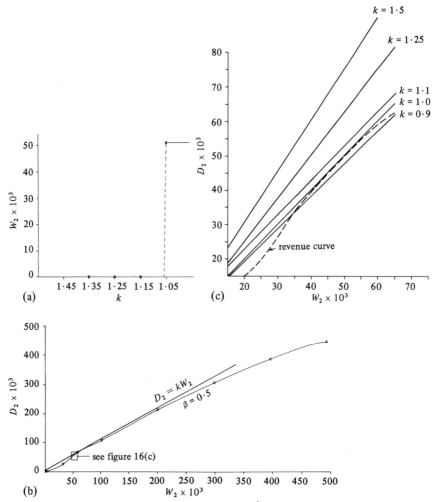

Figure 16. An example of the use of assumption 1′, for zone 2 with $\beta = 0 \cdot 5$ and $\alpha = 1 \cdot 3$. Note that in (b) $D_2 = kW_2$ is drawn for $W = 1 \cdot 8 \times 10^6$ and $W_2 = 50\,988$, and therefore appears as a straight line. The straight lines in (c) are the lines $D_2 = kW_2$ for various k.

programme, we can then input this set as in assumption 1', though with $W_j^{init} = W_j^{MP}$. Then we can change W_j very slightly around W_j^{init} to obtain a small part of the revenue curve. The assumption is that we are varying W and hence k only very slightly and that this would not perturb the mathematical programme to any great extent. We can then compare the revenue curve with the $D_j = kW_j$ curve.

We present an example of assumption 1' in figure 16. The jump shown in figure 16(a) involves a jump from $W_2 = 0$ to $W_2 = 50988$ for a small change in k ($\alpha = 1\cdot3$). A small jump was chosen because it would not greatly affect the overall W_l pattern. The revenue curve [figure 16(b)] shows that, for assumption 1', k_j^{crit} is located between $W_2 = 50000$ and $W_2 = 100000$. If we focus our attention on what is happening as the slope of the $D_j = kW_j$ curve changes, more precisely, as k decreases from $1\cdot5$ to 1, assuming that the revenue curve remains constant [figure 16(c)], it can be seen that in the vicinity of $k = 1\cdot05$ the $D_j = kW_j$ curve crosses the revenue curve around $W_j = 50000$. This suggests that the jump we are experiencing is in fact a jump from the lower stable point ($W_2 = 0$) to the upper stable point, as outlined earlier, for a small change in k. Given that the mathematical programme would almost inevitably have produced a slightly different analysis we can tentatively infer that we are experiencing a jump caused by passing through k_j^{crit}; and this confirms our general argument in spite of the difficulties outlined in section 4.

Assumption 3 produces a slightly different analysis. As W_j varies slightly the W_l pattern is free to change, and this may affect the revenue pattern. We may expect therefore a different revenue curve than under assumption 1', although the variation should not be great. Early experiments suggest that this is in fact the case. It is also worth noting that the D_j produced for a given W_j by use of a spatial-interaction model will not be *exactly* the same as that produced with the mathematical programme, but the correlation between the two sets of D_js should be very high (in the order of $r^2 = 0\cdot99$—see Coelho and Wilson, 1976).

6.5 Further problems
It can easily be observed from constraint equation (8) that if a jump occurs in any zone then at least one other zone must exhibit jump behaviour. The problem this raises is that of selecting the zone that is experiencing a 'first-order' jump, that is, one caused by satisfying one of the several conditions for jumps as outlined in section 3, and not behaviour triggered by a jump in another zone. In the example given in section 6.4 the jump was only small and its effects were spread throughout the system. However, in the more general case this may not be so. In theory then we have to examine the revenue and $D_j = kW_j$ curves for each zone under a variety of different assumptions. This is clearly a laborious and time-consuming task. An alternative approach would be to develop a model that explicitly introduced demand *and* supply mechanisms so as to

determine the total stock, W, endogenously within the model, thus removing constraint (8). Then jumps could occur in response to the economic mechanisms outlined earlier *without* the necessity of any concomitant jumps arising in other zones.

7 Concluding comments and problems for further research

At least three kinds of further research tasks can be identified. First there are difficult mathematical problems to be coped with. It is still not entirely clear that jumps can be interpreted by use of the mechanism of Harris and Wilson (1978) and of this paper. There is, for example, the possibility of some jumps being caused by 'constraint catastrophes' associated with the mathematical programme (see Poston and Stewart, 1978, for a general discussion of this). There are also possible convexity problems for the $\alpha > 1$ case, though we have tried to eliminate the possibility that jumps are not caused by movements from a local optimum to a global optimum by noting that the objective function only changes slightly. Further we have also discovered, and presented, a jump for the $\alpha = 1$ case where the convexity of the objective function is not in doubt. Another kind of mathematical problem concerns the possibility of cusp or swallowtail catastrophes existing since two or three parameters (k, α, and β say) are involved—though in this case, as our analysis showed, they are not all independent. If terms like the $e_i P_i$ are allowed to vary, then we move into the realm of higher-order catastrophes.

The second kind of research task involves improving the numerical experiments. We now feel that it may be better to use more zones—so that a jump in one zone does not have such a dramatic effect on others— and also that it may be better to use a square grid system and controlled hypothetical data. (On the other hand, there may be advantages in exploring a two-zone system also.)

Third, as we noted at the outset of this section, research should take us into more complicated models in which the model of this paper will become one submodel. Jumps in one submodel will then trigger jumps in others.

Perhaps the main general conclusion to be drawn from this paper is that, where a theoretical base is complicated, the carrying out of numerical experiments is a valuable additional *theoretical* tool. Problems are thrown into sharp focus and this can lead to new theoretical developments. More specifically, a lot of evidence has been accumulated that a well-known urban model does implicitly contain jump behaviour in its dynamics. This in itself has generated new research possibilities, as we briefly noted. But we should also be aware that this is one submodel within a more complex comprehensive model. For example, we noted the possible dependence of W_j behaviour on the $e_i P_i$ pattern; but the P_i are themselves dependent on the W_j—see Wilson (1978) for a more extended discussion of this point. This implies that the task of unravelling the complexities of the dynamics of urban spatial structure as a whole is a particularly difficult one which will take a lot of scientific effort.

Acknowledgements. The authors wish to thank Professor P Huard and Dr J Guigou, of Électricité de France, for supplying the reduced-gradient program.

References

Coelho J D, 1977 "The use of mathematical optimisation methods in model based land use planning: an application to the new town of Santo André" Ph D thesis, School of Geography, University of Leeds, Leeds

Coelho J D, Wilson A G, 1976 "The optimum location and size of shopping centres" *Regional Studies* **10** 413-421

Guigou J, 1975 "Note d'utilization du code GR" Service Informatique et Mathematique Appliquées, Direction des Études et Recherche, Électricité de France, Paris

Harris B, Wilson A G, 1978 "Equilibrium values and dynamics of attractiveness terms in production-constrained spatial-interaction models" *Environment and Planning A* **10** 371-388

Huff D L, 1964 "Defining and estimating a trading area" *Journal of Marketing* **28** 37-38

Lakshmanan T R, Hansen W G, 1965 "A retail market potential model" *Journal of the American Institute of Planners* **31** 134-143

Leonardi G, 1978 "Optimum facility location by accessibility maximising" *Environment and Planning A* **10** 1287-1305

Poston T, Stewart I, 1978 *Catastrophe Theory and Its Applications* (Pitman, London)

Poston T, Wilson A G, 1977 "Facility size versus distance travelled: urban services and the fold catastrophe" *Environment and Planning A* **9** 681-686

Thom R, 1975 *Structural Stability and Morphogenesis* (Benjamin, New York)

White R W, 1977 "Dynamic central place theory: results of a simulation approach" *Geographical Analysis* **9** 226-243

Wilson A G, 1978 "Spatial interaction and settlement structure: towards an explicit central place theory" in *Spatial Interaction Theory and Planning Models* Eds A Karlqvist, L Lundqvist, F Snickars, J W Weibull (North-Holland, Amsterdam) pp 137-156

Zahler R S, Sussman H J, 1977 "Claims and accomplishments of applied catastrophe theory" *Nature* **269** 759-763

A Mathematical-programming Framework for the Optimal Location of Spatially Interacting Activities: Theory and Algorithms

G LEONARDI
Politecnico di Torino

1 Introduction

The purpose of this paper is to provide a unified theoretical and operational approach to the problem of optimizing the location of a set of spatially interacting activities. Many practical problems share the structure of a system of spatially interacting activities. In section 2 of this paper two illustrative examples are considered: a Lowry-like system, with the well-known basic-employment–residence–retail-activity interactions; and a multilevel health-care system, where interactions take place among different levels of health-care activities.

The choice of the two examples is due to my own personal experience, but it should not be taken as restrictive. Indeed the mathematical framework and the computational tools presented here can be applied to the optimization of the spatial pattern of any system sharing the following general features:

(1) the system possesses a set of different kinds of activities;
(2) interactions take place among activities according to a linear or input–output structure;
(3) interactions among activities are disaggregated over space according to a production-constrained spatial-interaction model.

It should be stressed from the start that the two examples discussed in section 2 are intended to aid understanding of the structure of the system to be studied and are not the main focus of the paper. This will be found in section 3, where the general problem of optimizing a system of spatially interacting activities will be stated in mathematical terms and the necessary and sufficient conditions for its solution will be analysed, and in section 4, where a class of computational algorithms is developed and discussed.

2 The system to be studied

A great variety of practical situations in planning can be seen as a set of interacting activities. Interactions among activities can be flows of people, goods, or money, and they are usually adequately modelled by a constant-coefficient input–output matrix—that is, by a linear structure. Flows travel over space, and the way they do so is usually adequately modelled by a spatial-interaction or gravity model.

A typical planning problem associated with such a system is deciding how much of each activity should be located in each zone of a given set in order to attain the maximum value of some measure of benefit.

This is the planning problem to which the rest of this paper is devoted, and we shall need a precise mathematical formulation of the systems defined in section 1 if we want to translate it into mathematical-programming terms. A general mathematical model of a system of spatially interacting activities will be given in section 2.3. Before working out its mathematical details, however, it will be useful to present two examples of well-known systems in the hope that this will make the general abstraction easier to grasp. This is the purpose of sections 2.1 and 2.2.

2.1 Example 1: a spatial-interaction and activity system

It is assumed that everyone is familiar with Lowry-like modelling of spatial-interaction and activity (SIA) models. We shall consider a simplified version of an SIA model, consisting of just three activities—housing, basic activities, and retail (nonbasic) activities.

Assuming the usual hypotheses of economic-base theory (Richardson, 1969), we are led to the following set of equations for the state variable of our system:

$$H_j = E_j^b + \alpha \sum_k R_k q_{kj} , \qquad \forall j , \tag{1}$$

$$R_j = \beta \sum_k H_k p_{kj} , \qquad \forall j , \tag{2}$$

where

H_j is the demand for housing from zone j (that is, total employment in zone j);

E_j^b is basic employment in zone j;

R_j is the total demand for retail goods in zone j, in terms of cash flow;

q_{kj} is the probability that the retail demand from zone k will be supplied by going shopping in zone j;

p_{kj} is the probability that a householder working in zone k will choose a residence in zone j; and

α, β are constants.

In other words, equation (1) says that housing demand in each zone is given by the sum of basic and nonbasic employment, the latter being proportional to the output of retail activity; equation (2) says that retail demand in each zone is proportional to the number of households resident in it.

The probabilities q_{kj} and p_{kj} are usually assumed to be given by the production-constrained spatial-interaction models (see Wilson, 1971)

$$q_{kj} = \frac{x_j^a f_{kj}}{\sum_j x_j^a f_{kj}} \qquad \text{and} \qquad p_{kj} = \frac{y_j^b g_{kj}}{\sum_j y_j^b g_{kj}} , \tag{3}$$

where

x_j, y_j are respectively measures of retail and housing attractiveness in zone j;

f_{kj}, g_{kj} are respectively measures of impedance to home-to-shopping and
home-to-work travelling; and
a, b are constants.
The impedance measures are usually taken to be given by

$$f_{kj} = \exp(-\gamma c_{kj}) \quad \text{and} \quad g_{kj} = \exp(-\delta c_{kj}), \quad (4)$$

where c_{kj} is the travel cost between zones k and j, and γ and δ are
positive constants.

Formulae (1)–(4) are often taken as a basis for simulating the impact
of alternative planning policies, with the E_j^b as input and the x_j and y_j as
control variables. However, the set of alternative values for the x_j and y_j
to be tested by simulation is usually built by intuition, and no true
optimization can be carried out on it.

Instead here an attempt will be made to place the SIA model in a
mathematical-programming framework [1]. Accordingly it will be assumed
that values for the x_j and y_j will be chosen to maximize a given objective
function. For reasons that will become clear later, it is proposed to use
as the objective function the log-accessibility function as defined in
Leonardi (1978), which for present purposes assumes the form

$$\Psi(x,y) = \sum_i R_i \ln \left(\sum_j x_j^a f_{ij} \right) + \sum_i H_i \ln \left(\sum_j y_j^b g_{ij} \right), \quad (5)$$

where x and y are vectors whose components are the x_j and y_j respectively.
This can be interpreted as accessibility of retail demand to retail activities
plus accessibility of housing demand (workers) to residences. If x_j is
interpreted as the size of the shopping centre in zone j, and y_j as the
number of residences in zone j, it is reasonable to assume that the x_j and
y_j are subject to some constraints; these will be summarized by writing

$$(x,y) \in C, \quad (6)$$

where C is some compact subset of an aptly defined vector space.

To conclude, the following SIA programming problem can be formulated

$$\underset{\{x,y\}}{\text{maximize}} \ \Psi(x,y) \quad (7)$$

subject to

$$(x,y) \in C \quad (8)$$

and under the assumption that equations (1)–(3) hold.

Because of equations (1)–(3), the form of the functional dependence of
Ψ on the x_j and y_j cannot be written explicitly, and this is true also for

[1] This has already been done for simulation by use of extremal principles (see
Wilson, 1977, appendix 2, for example). Here a quite different approach will be
pursued—that is, optimization to achieve some planning goal. However, it will be
seen later that the objective function in this paper, accessibility, is closely related to
the function used in simulation, consumer surplus.

the derivatives of Ψ. We will see later how this difficulty can be overcome by some numerical devices.

2.2 Example 2: a health-care system

The evolution of states of health in a given population can be modelled as a Markov process (see Chiang, 1968, for instance) in which the 'illness state' of each patient undergoes a sequence of changes until recovery or death is reached. The set of illness states is, or can be defined to be, a discrete and finite set; furthermore, the simplifying assumption that there is a one-to-one mapping between the set of illness states and a set of health-care facilities of different kinds can be introduced. We are thus led to the problem of optimally locating and sizing health-care facilities according to some given objective function.

This is the kind of problem investigated by Bertuglia and Leonardi (1978), for which they give a theoretical and operational framework that will be briefly sketched here. Bertuglia and Leonardi consider a system whose steady state is determined by the set of equations

$$P_{nj} = Q_{nj} + \sum_m \pi_{mn} \sum_i P_{mi} q_{ij}^m , \qquad \forall j, n , \tag{9}$$

where

P_{nj} is the flow of people in zone j undergoing a change towards the nth illness state;

Q_{nj} is the flow of people in zone j who enter the illness sequence at the nth state;

π_{mn} is the probability of going from illness state m to illness state n; and

q_{ij}^m is the probability, for people in zone i going towards the mth illness state, of choosing the health-care facility for the mth state in zone j.

As usual it is assumed that the probabilities q_{ij}^m are given by

$$q_{ij}^m = \frac{x_{mj}^{\alpha_m} f_{ij}^m}{\sum_j x_{mj}^{\alpha_m} f_{ij}^m} , \tag{10}$$

where the meanings of the symbols are analogous to those defined for equations (3).

In other words, equations (9) say that demand for health-care facilities in each zone, relative to each illness state, is given by the sum of two terms: the number of people who start the illness sequence with the given illness state, and the number of people who are already in the illness sequence and have the given illness state as their next step.

As in example 1, the health-care problem will be placed in a mathematical-programming framework. That is, we want to choose values for the x_{mj}, the sizes of each kind of facility m in each zone j, so that a given objective function attains its maximum. Again the log-accessibility function is introduced, which was defined by Bertuglia and Leonardi (1978) for this problem as

$$\Psi(x) = \sum_{n,i} P_{ni} \ln \left(\sum x_{nj}^{\alpha_n} f_{ij}^n \right) ,$$ (11)

where x stands for the array of the x_{nj}. If C is the feasible set defined by the constraints on x, we have the following programming problem:

$$\underset{x}{\text{maximize }} \Psi(x)$$ (12)

subject to

$$x \in C$$ (13)

and under the assumption that equations (9) and (10) hold.

Again equations (9) and (10) determine a complicated form of the function $\Psi(x)$ which cannot be written in closed form. As already observed in example 1, we have to resort to some numerical technique to compute the values of Ψ and of its derivatives.

2.3 Formal structure of a generalized SIA system

We are now ready to abstract from these two examples to give a general mathematical framework for what will be called a generalized SIA system. In loose terms, by a generalized SIA system is meant a system defined by a set of different activities among which spatial interactions take place. No limitation will be placed on the kind and number of activities, flows, and possible interactions, since we are building a general formal structure. Therefore, both the Lowry-like SIA model in example 1 and the health-care system in example 2 are generalized SIA systems.

A generalized SIA system is, for our purposes, a system whose steady-state behaviour is governed by the following set of simultaneous linear equations:

$$P_{nj} = Q_{nj} + \sum_m \pi_{mn} \sum_i P_{mi} q_{ij}^m , \qquad \forall j, n ,$$ (14)

where
P_{nj} is the total flow from zone j to activity n;
Q_{nj} is the input, or exogenous[2] flow, from zone j to activity n;
q_{ij}^m is the probability that the flow from zone i to activity m goes into zone j; and
π_{mn} is a constant.
It will generally be assumed that

$$q_{ij}^m \geqslant 0 , \qquad \forall i, j, m ,$$ (15)

$$\sum_j q_{ij}^m = 1 , \qquad \forall i, m ,$$ (16)

---

[2] It is exogenous with respect to the system—that is, it does not come from any one of the activities in the system.

and

$$\pi_{mn} \geqslant 0 \, , \qquad \forall m, n \, . \tag{17}$$

The aggregated counterpart of equation (14) can be obtained by summing it over the zones j. If

$$T_n = \sum_j P_{nj} \, , \qquad \text{the total flow towards activity } n \, , \tag{18}$$

and

$$I_n = \sum_j g_{nj} \, , \qquad \text{the total input to activity } n \, , \tag{19}$$

we have

$$T_n = I_n + \sum_m T_m \pi_{mn} \, , \qquad \forall n \, . \tag{20}$$

Equations (20) are similar to an input–output model, so that we can call the π_{mn} the input–output coefficients between the activities [3]. We can thus say that equations (14) represent a spatial disaggregation of an input–output model like that given by equations (20).

Up to this point no assumption has been made on the form of the q_{ij}^m. From now on it will be assumed that they are given by the production-constrained spatial-interaction models

$$q_{ij}^m = \frac{W_{mj}^{\alpha_m} h_{ij}^m}{\sum_j W_{mj}^{\alpha_m} h_{ij}^m} \, , \qquad \forall i, j, m \, , \tag{21}$$

where

W_{mj} is a measure of the size, or attractiveness, of activity m in zone j;
h_{ij}^m is a measure of impedance to travel from zone i to activity m in zone j; and
α_m is a parameter.

The impedance measure h_{ij}^m is usually assumed to be of the form

$$h_{ij}^m = \exp(-\lambda_m c_{ij}) \, , \tag{22}$$

where c_{ij} is the cost of travel from zone i to zone j and λ_m is a parameter. However, most of the results of this paper do not depend on this assumption.

The values of P_{nj} can be computed either by matrix methods or by the following successive-approximation scheme:

$$P_{nj}^{(N+1)} = Q_{nj} + \sum_m \pi_{mn} \sum_i P_{mi}^{(N)} q_{ij}^m \, . \tag{23}$$

From equations (21) and (23) an important property of P_{nj} can be deduced. If we define the vectors

$$W_m = (W_{mj}) \, , \qquad \forall m \, , \tag{24}$$

[3] The similarity is only algebraic; in general one should not confuse equations (20) with an input–output model in the Leontief sense.

we see at once, from equation (21), that q_{ij}^m is homogeneous of degree zero with respect to W_m; that is,

$$q_{ij}^m(\eta W_m) = q_{ij}^m(W_m) , \tag{25}$$

for any scalar η, where the parentheses denote a functional relationship. But by induction on formula (23) we see immediately that also every successive approximation $P_{nj}^{(N)}$ is homogeneous of degree zero with respect to each vector W_m. This must be true also as $N \to \infty$; but

$$\lim_{N \to \infty} P_{nj}^{(N)} = P_{nj} , \tag{26}$$

and hence we may conclude that the P_{nj} are homogeneous functions of degree zero of the vectors W_m. From this and from Euler's theorem for homogeneous functions it follows that

$$\sum_k \frac{\partial P_{nj}}{\partial W_{mk}} W_{mk} = 0 , \qquad \forall j, m, n . \tag{27}$$

This property will be very useful later.

We shall also need a way to compute the derivatives of the P_{nj}. To this end, we differentiate both sides of equations (14) to get

$$\frac{\partial P_{nj}}{\partial W_{lk}} = \sum_m \pi_{mn} \sum_i \frac{\partial P_{mi}}{\partial W_{lk}} q_{ij}^m + \pi_{ln} \sum_i P_{li} \frac{\partial q_{ij}^l}{\partial W_{lk}} , \qquad \forall j, k, l, n . \tag{28}$$

This is a set of equations for the unknown derivatives, and can be solved either by matrix methods or by successive approximations according to the formulae

$$Y_{nj, lk}^{(N+1)} = A_{nj, lk} + \sum_m \pi_{mn} \sum_i Y_{mi, lk}^{(N)} q_{ij}^m , \qquad \forall j, k, l, n , \tag{29}$$

where $Y_{nj, lk}^{(N)}$ is the Nth approximation to $\partial P_{nj}/\partial W_{lk}$, and

$$A_{nj, lk} = \pi_{ln} \sum_i P_{li} \frac{\partial q_{ij}^l}{\partial W_{lk}} , \tag{30}$$

which is a known constant quantity provided the P_{lj} have already been computed (the derivative $\partial q_{ij}^l/\partial W_{lk}$ can be easily computed).

To conclude this section, notice how examples 1 and 2 are actually special cases of equations (14). Equations (1) and (2) form a system of the same form as equations (14), where $m, n = 1$ (retail), 2 (housing); $\pi_{12} = \alpha$, $\pi_{21} = \beta$, $\pi_{11} = \pi_{22} = 0$; $Q_{1j} = 0$, $Q_{2j} = E_j^b$. Equations (9) are obviously of the same form as equations (14) since even the same symbols are used; the only difference is that in the general case the input–output coefficients, π_{mn}, need not be probabilities as in equations (9).

3 Some mathematical-programming problems
If we want to optimize a generalized SIA system, we are faced with the problem of determining simultaneously the size and location of many

different activities—that is, we are faced with a multifacility-location problem. However, since much of the theory and many of the tools we need are generalizations of those present in problems of single-facility location, such problems will be briefly reviewed here.

3.1 Optimum location of a single facility
In Leonardi (1978) the following optimum-location problem is considered:

$$\text{maximize } \Psi = \sum_i P_i \ln \left(\sum_j W_j^\alpha h_{ij} \right) \qquad \qquad (31)$$
$$\{W_j\}$$

subject to

$$\sum_j c_j W_j^\beta = B \qquad \qquad (32)$$

and

$$W_j \geq 0, \qquad \forall j, \qquad \qquad (33)$$

where

P_i is the total demand in zone i;
W_j is the size of the facility in zone j;
h_{ij} is a measure of impedance to travel from zone i to zone j;
B is the total budget; and
c_j, α, β are parameters.

Constraint (32) is a total-budget constraint; cost functions with nonunity elasticity, β, are generally allowed for because of possible scale economies. The function Ψ defined in equation (31) is the log-accessibility function first used by Loenardi (1973). In Leonardi (1978) it is shown that this function is closely related to the Coelho and Williams (1979) definition of consumer surplus. Indeed it can be easily proved that consumer surplus is log-accessibility up to a linear transformation which does not affect maximization; this is true provided the production-constrained spatial-interaction model is assumed to hold.

As an aside, it is interesting to note that, in Coelho and Wilson's (1976) shopping model, consumer surplus is used both as an extremal principle to embed the spatial-interaction model and as an objective function to plan the optimum location and size of shopping centres. Thus, after the embedding, the problem of Coelho and Wilson (1976) is equivalent to the problem of Leonardi (1978).

In Leonardi (1978) it is also shown that problem (31)–(33) can be reduced to the following standard form:

$$\text{maximize } \Psi = \sum_i p_i \ln \left(\sum_j x_j^\theta f_{ij} \right) \qquad \qquad (34)$$
$$\{x_j\}$$

subject to

$$\sum_j x_j = 1 \qquad \qquad (35)$$

and

$$x_j \geq 0, \qquad \forall j, \tag{36}$$

where the following transformations have been carried out:

$$p_i = \frac{P_i}{\sum_i P_i}, \qquad \forall i, \tag{37}$$

$$x_j = \frac{c_j W_j^\beta}{B}, \qquad \forall j, \tag{38}$$

$$\theta = \frac{\alpha}{\beta}, \tag{39}$$

and

$$f_{ij} = \frac{h_{ij}}{c_j^\theta}. \tag{40}$$

It can be shown (see Leonardi, 1978) that the optimal point of problem (34)-(36) is the solution to the following set of equations:

$$D_j = x_j, \qquad \forall j, \tag{41}$$

where

$$D_j = \sum_i p_i \frac{x_j^\theta f_{ij}}{\sum_j x_j^\theta f_{ij}} \tag{42}$$

is the flow to zone j as a fraction of total flow. Each of equations (41) is nothing but a special form of the Harris balancing condition between attracted flow and facility size (Harris, 1964; Harris and Wilson, 1978), which can be solved iteratively according to the usual scheme:

$$x_j^{(N+1)} = D_j^{(N)}. \tag{43}$$

However, Leonardi (1978) suggests that some improvement in the optimization algorithm could be obtained by using a feasible-direction scheme; that is,

$$x_j^{(N+1)} = x_j^{(N)} + \tau [D_j^{(N)} - x_j^{(N)}], \tag{44}$$

where τ is chosen to maximize Ψ along the direction $D_j^{(N)} - x_j^{(N)}$.

3.2 Multifacility optimum location
The multifacility problem analogous to that treated in section 3.1 is

$$\underset{\{W_{nj}, B_n\}}{\text{maximize}} \ \Psi = \sum_{n,i} P_{ni} \ln \left(\sum_j W_{nj}^{\alpha_n} h_{ij}^n \right) \tag{45}$$

subject to

$$\sum_j c_{nj} W_{nj}^{\beta_n} = B_n , \qquad \forall n , \tag{46}$$

$$\sum_n B_n = B , \tag{47}$$

and

$$B_n, W_{nj} \geqslant 0 , \qquad \forall j, n , \tag{48}$$

where the P_{ni} are equilibrium-state variables of a generalized SIA system, as defined by equation (14); and

W_{nj} is the size of activity n in zone j;

h_{ij}^n is a measure of impedance to travel from zone i to zone j towards activity n;

B_n is the total budget available for activity n;

B is the total budget for the whole system; and

$c_{nj}, \alpha_n, \beta_n$ are parameters.

It is shown by Bertuglia and Leonardi (1978) that problems like problem (45)–(48) can be reduced to a standard form, as with the single-facility problem. When this transformation is carried out, a useful separability property is revealed by which the programme can be split in two independent subprogrammes:

(1) optimum budget allocation among activities—that is,

$$\underset{\{B_n\}}{\text{maximize}} \, \Phi = \sum_n T_n \theta_n \ln B_n \tag{49}$$

subject to

$$\sum_n B_n = B \tag{50}$$

and

$$B_n \geqslant 0 , \qquad \forall n , \tag{51}$$

where

$$\theta_n = \frac{\alpha_n}{\beta_n} \tag{52}$$

and the T_n are the solutions to equations (20);

(2) optimum location and size of facilities—that is,

$$\underset{\{x_{nj}\}}{\text{maximize}} \, \Psi = \sum_{n, i} P_{ni} \ln \left(\sum_j x_{nj}^{\theta_n} f_{ij}^n \right) \tag{53}$$

subject to

$$\sum_j x_{nj} = 1 , \qquad \forall n , \tag{54}$$

and

$$x_{nj} \geqslant 0 , \qquad \forall j, n , \tag{55}$$

where

$$\theta_n = \frac{\alpha_n}{\beta_n} , \qquad \forall n , \tag{56}$$

$$x_{nj} = \frac{c_{nj} W_{nj}^{\beta_n}}{B_n} , \qquad \forall j, n , \tag{57}$$

and

$$f_{ij}^n = \frac{h_{ij}^n}{c_{nj}^{\theta_n}} , \qquad \forall i, j, n . \tag{58}$$

Now for subproblem (1) the optimal solution is trivial:

$$B_n = B \frac{T_n \theta_n}{\sum_n T_n \theta_n} , \qquad \forall n . \tag{59}$$

This is an intuitively reasonable rule since it says that we should allocate the total budget among the activities proportionally to their total demand, T_n, and to the ratio of the attracted-flow elasticity to the cost elasticity, θ_n.

Subproblem (2) gives rise to the Kuhn–Tucker conditions [see, for instance, Mangasarian (1969) for a detailed statement and discussion of the Kuhn–Tucker theorem]

$$\frac{\partial \Psi}{\partial x_{mk}} = \mu_m - \epsilon_{mk} , \qquad \forall k, m , \tag{60}$$

$$\epsilon_{mk} x_{mk} = 0 , \qquad \forall k, m , \tag{61}$$

and

$$\epsilon_{mk} \geq 0 , \qquad \forall k, m , \tag{62}$$

where μ_m and ϵ_{mk} are the Lagrangian multipliers corresponding to budget constraints (54) and to nonnegativity constraints (55) respectively. The derivatives of Ψ are

$$\frac{\partial \Psi}{\partial x_{mk}} = \theta_m \frac{D_{mk}}{x_{mk}} + \sum_{n,i} \frac{\partial P_{ni}}{\partial x_{mk}} \ln \left(\sum_j x_{nj}^{\theta_n} f_{ij}^n \right) , \qquad \forall k, m , \tag{63}$$

where

$$D_{mk} = \sum_i P_{mi} \frac{x_{mk}^{\theta_m} f_{ik}^m}{\sum_k x_{mk}^{\theta_m} f_{ik}^m} \tag{64}$$

is the flow to activities m in zone k.

We can easily calculate the value of the multipliers μ_m. If we multiply both sides of equations (60) by x_{mk} and sum over k, by use of complementarity conditions (61) and constraints (54) we have

$$\sum_k \frac{\partial \Psi}{\partial x_{mk}} x_{mk} = \mu_m , \qquad \forall m ; \tag{65}$$

that is, from equations (63),

$$\theta_m \sum_k D_{mk} + \sum_{n,i} \left(\sum_k \frac{\partial P_{ni}}{\partial x_{mk}} x_{mk} \right) \ln \left(\sum_j x_{nj}^{\theta_n} f_{ij}^n \right) = \mu_m .$$ (66)

Now, from equations (64) and (18) we have

$$\sum_k D_{mk} = \sum_i P_{mi} = T_m ;$$ (67)

on the other hand, from property (27) we have [4]

$$\sum_{n,i} \left(\sum_k \frac{\partial P_{ni}}{\partial x_{mk}} x_{mk} \right) \ln \left(\sum_j x_{nj}^{\theta_n} f_{ij}^n \right) = 0 .$$ (68)

It follows that equation (66) becomes

$$\theta_m T_m = \mu_m .$$ (69)

One further remark concludes this section. In actual applications the allocation of the total budget among the activities is not necessarily determined by rule (59). We can also have more constrained formulations of the programming problem, in which the B_n are no longer control variables but rather are given input quantities. This is the case when the B_n are fixed by criteria other than those of optimum location, possibly by a higher planning level, such as regional economic planning. This paper will not be concerned with the different ways the B_n can be determined or given; one just needs to note that, in the more constrained case, the problem reduces to subprogramme (2) only.

3.3 Land-availability constraints

It will now be assumed that there are additional constraints due to limited availability of usable land. To encompass these constraints, the earlier formulation will be changed slightly. Required land will be adopted as a measure of the size of each facility; it will be tacitly assumed that this measure is linearly or almost linearly related to the other size measures, such as volume or fraction of total budget, so that the same form of generalized SIA model will hold (after the necessary transformations have been carried out). Some generality will also be traded off for mathematical tractability by considering linear constraints both for the budget and for the land.

The remark made at the end of section 3.2 indicates that there can be two cases, depending on whether the budgets for each activity are control variables or given quantities. In the first case the programming problem is

$$\underset{\{x_{nj}\}}{\text{maximize}} \ \Psi = \sum_{n,i} P_{ni} \sum_j x_{nj}^{\theta_n} f_{ij}^n$$ (70)

---

[4] Property (27) was proved for the W_{mk} variables, but it obviously holds for the x_{mk} variables too.

subject to

$$\sum_{n,j} c_{nj} x_{nj} = B \ , \tag{71}$$

$$\sum_{n} x_{nj} \leqslant S_j \ , \qquad \forall j \ , \tag{72}$$

and

$$x_{nj} \geqslant 0 \ , \qquad \forall j, n \ , \tag{73}$$

where
c_{nj} is the unit cost for activity n in zone j;
x_{nj} is the land used for activity n in zone j;
B is the total budget; and
S_j is the total available land in zone j.
In the second case the programming problem is

$$\underset{\{x_{nj}\}}{\text{maximize }} \Psi \tag{74}$$

subject to

$$\sum_{j} c_{nj} x_{nj} = B_n \ , \qquad \forall n \ , \tag{75}$$

$$\sum_{n} x_{nj} \leqslant S_j \ , \qquad \forall j \ , \tag{76}$$

and

$$x_{nj} \geqslant 0 \ , \qquad \forall j, n \ , \tag{77}$$

where the variables are defined as before except that B_n is the budget for activity n.

Unfortunately no further transformation can be usefully performed on problems (70)-(73) and (74)-(77). In particular no separability property can be found. This is due to land constraints, which tie together budget allocation and facility location.

The conditions to be met by the optimal solution points to these two problems are as follows. For problem (70)-(73) the Kuhn–Tucker conditions are

$$\Psi_{nj} = c_{nj}\mu + \nu_j - \epsilon_{nj} \ , \qquad \forall j, n \ , \tag{78}$$

$$\nu_j \left(S_j - \sum_{n} x_{nj} \right) = 0 \ , \qquad \forall j \ , \tag{79}$$

$$\epsilon_{nj} x_{nj} = 0 \ , \qquad \forall j, n \ , \tag{80}$$

and

$$\nu_j, \epsilon_{nj} \geqslant 0 \ , \qquad \forall j, n \ , \tag{81}$$

where
Ψ_{nj} is the derivative of Ψ with respect to x_{nj} [see formula (63) for the detailed expression];
μ is the multiplier associated with budget constraint (71);
ν_j is the multiplier associated with land constraint (72) for zone j;
ϵ_{nj} is the multiplier associated with nonnegativity constraint (73) for activity n in zone j.

For problem (74)–(77) the Kuhn–Tucker conditions are

$$\Psi_{nj} = c_{nj}\mu_n + \nu_j - \epsilon_{nj} , \qquad \forall j, n , \tag{82}$$

$$\nu_j \left(S_j - \sum_n x_{nj} \right) = 0 , \qquad \forall j , \tag{83}$$

$$\epsilon_{nj} x_{nj} = 0 , \qquad \forall j, n , \tag{84}$$

and

$$\nu_j , \epsilon_{nj} \geqslant 0 , \qquad \forall j, n , \tag{85}$$

where the symbols are defined as before except that μ_n is the multiplier associated with budget constraint (75) for activity n.

Unlike the case treated in section 3.2, the values for the multipliers cannot be calculated explicitly. The problem must be tackled with some numerical technique, and this is the subject of section 4.

4 The balancing algorithm and its generalizations
In this section some algorithms will be given for solving the problems stated in sections 3.1, 3.2, and 3.3. Whereas the algorithm for section 3.1 is well-known, the ones for sections 3.2 and 3.3 are new. But, as will be shown, they can be considered as generalizations of the algorithm for section 3.1.

4.1 Balancing algorithm for the single-facility-location problem
In section 3.1 the following generalization of Harris's (1964) classical flow–capacity balancing algorithm was suggested:

$$x_j^{(N+1)} = x_j^{(N)} + \tau[D_j^{(N)} - x_j^{(N)}] . \tag{86}$$

Here it will be given a new derivation, which will be easy to generalize in the more complicated cases.

We start from the Kuhn–Tucker conditions of problem (34)–(36), which are

$$\Psi_j = \mu + \epsilon_j , \qquad \forall j , \tag{87}$$

$$\epsilon_j x_j = 0 , \qquad \forall j , \tag{88}$$

and

$$\epsilon_j \geqslant 0 , \qquad \forall j , \tag{89}$$

where
Ψ_j is the derivative of Ψ with respect to x_j;

$$\Psi_j = \frac{\partial \Psi}{\partial x_j} = \frac{D_j}{x_j} \; ; \tag{90}$$

μ is the multiplier associated with constraint (35); and
ϵ_j is the multiplier associated with constraint (36) for zone j.
Since the Kuhn–Tucker conditions must be satisfied at the optimal point,
an algorithm can be devised where, given the current approximation for
the x_j, one tries to compute the multipliers which satisfy equations (87)
as closely as possible.

A natural way of measuring closeness is total squared deviation. We
are thus led to solve the least-squares problem

$$\underset{\{x_j\}}{\text{minimize}} \, Z = \sum_j x_j (\Psi_j - \mu)^2 \; ; \tag{91}$$

that is, we need to minimize the sum of squared deviations, weighted with
the x_j variables [note that, because of multiplication by x_j and
complementarity conditions (88), the multipliers ϵ_j have disappeared].
Minimizing Z implies that

$$\frac{\partial Z}{\partial \mu} = -2 \sum_j x_j (\Psi_j - \mu) = 0 \; ; \tag{92}$$

that is, by use of constraint (35),

$$\sum_j x_j \Psi_j = \mu \, . \tag{93}$$

But

$$\sum_j x_j \Psi_j = \sum_j D_j = 1 \, , \tag{94}$$

so that

$$\mu = 1 \, . \tag{95}$$

Indeed, from section 3.1, we know that this is the true value for μ at the
optimal point.

From equations (91) and (92) it follows that

$$Z = \sum_j x_j (\Psi_j - \mu) \Psi_j - \sum_j x_j (\Psi_j - \mu) \mu = \sum_j x_j (\Psi_j - \mu) \Psi_j \, , \tag{96}$$

and this quantity is surely nonnegative, being a weighted sum of squares.
Thus, if d is direction vector with components

$$d_j = x_j (\Psi_j - \mu) \, , \tag{97}$$

the directional derivative of Ψ along d is

$$\nabla \Psi(d) = \sum_j x_j (\Psi_j - \mu) \Psi_j \geq 0 \, . \tag{98}$$

This means the value of Ψ increases as one moves along d; moreover d is also feasible (see Leonardi, 1978) since, from equation (92),

$$\sum_j d_j = 0 , \tag{99}$$

so that, for every point y computed by the formula

$$y = x + \tau d , \qquad \tau > 0 , \tag{100}$$

provided that x is feasible, we have

$$\sum_j y_j = \sum_j x_j + \tau \sum_j d_j = 1 . \tag{101}$$

These properties provide good theoretical justification for the use of algorithm (44).

The idea of using least squares to compute approximations to the multipliers is, to my knowledge, due to Fletcher (see, for instance, Fletcher, 1970), although the use of least squares is rather different here.

4.2 Algorithm for the multifacility-location problem with no land constraints

The method shown in section 4.1 will now be applied to problem (53)–(55). The Kuhn–Tucker conditions for this problem are conditions (60)–(62). In analogy with problem (91) we form the total squared deviation

$$Z = \sum_{n,j} x_{nj} (\Psi_{nj} - \mu_n)^2 , \tag{102}$$

where $\Psi_{nj} = \partial \Psi / \partial x_{nj}$. Minimizing Z implies that

$$\frac{\partial Z}{\partial \mu_n} = -2 \sum_j x_{nj} (\Psi_{nj} - \mu_n) = 0 , \qquad \forall n . \tag{103}$$

From this it follows, by use of constraints (54), that

$$\sum_j x_{nj} \Psi_{nj} = \mu_n , \qquad \forall n . \tag{104}$$

But from equations (18), (27), (63), and (64) we easily get

$$\sum_j x_{nj} \Psi_{nj} = \theta_n T_n , \qquad \forall n , \tag{105}$$

so that

$$\mu_n = \theta_n T_n , \qquad \forall n . \tag{106}$$

Indeed these are the values for the μ_n multipliers at the optimal point.

From equations (102) and (103) it follows that

$$Z = \sum_{n,j} x_{nj} (\Psi_{nj} - \mu_n) \Psi_{nj} - \sum_{n,j} x_{nj} (\Psi_{nj} - \mu_n) \mu_n = \sum_{n,j} x_{nj} (\Psi_{nj} - \mu_n) \Psi_{nj} , \tag{107}$$

and this is a nonnegative quantity, being a weighted sum of squares. In analogy with section 4.1, a feasible-direction algorithm can be defined based on the direction vector d with components

$$d_{nj} = x_{nj}(\Psi_{nj} - \mu_n) .$$ (108)

The proof of convenience and feasibility parallels the one given in section 4.1 and so will not be repeated here.

4.3 Algorithm for the multifacility-location problem with land constraints

We will now turn to problems of section 3.3, namely problems (70)-(73) and (74)-(77). The usual method cannot be used as it stands since it is defined for equality constraints only. To overcome this difficulty the inequality-constrained problems will be embedded in a sequence of equality-constrained ones, according to the "active set strategy" of Fletcher (1972) or the "manifold suboptimization" of Zangwill (1969). Each term of the sequence will then be treated by the method for equality constraints.

First the outer loop of the algorithm will be described. An iteration starts with the value x for the solution vector and the set L of zones where the land constraint is binding,

$$L = \left\{ j : \sum_n x_{nj} = S_j \right\} .$$ (109)

We shall solve the programming problem

maximize Ψ (110)

subject to constraint (71) or constraint (75), and

$$\sum_n x_{nj} = S_j , \qquad j \in L ,$$ (111)

and

$$x_{nj} \geqslant 0 , \qquad \forall j, n ,$$ (112)

which is equality-constrained and constitutes the inner loop of the algorithm (whose method of solution will be stated shortly). Call y the solution to this problem. There are two possible cases.

(1) y is infeasible for the inequality-constrained problem; that is

$$\sum_n x_{nj} > S_j , \qquad \text{for some } j \notin L ,$$ (113)

In this case take as a new x value the intersection of the line between x and y with the boundary of the feasible region. The new L will be the set of land constraints which are active at this intersection.

(2) y is feasible for the inequality-constrained problem. Along with y, the multipliers for constraints (111) have been computed; call these multipliers v_j. If all the v_j are nonnegative then clearly y is optimal for the inequality-constrained problem. If some v_j are negative, y will be the starting point for a new iteration. The active set L will be updated by removing from it the zone to which the least v_j value is associated.

We now come to the inner loop of the algorithm—that is, to the solution of programming problem (110)–(112). Straightforward application of the method already used in sections 4.1 and 4.2 yields the following algorithm: given a feasible point x, compute a better point y according to

$$y = x + \tau d , \tag{114}$$

where τ is chosen so as to maximize Ψ along d [subject to constraints (112)] and d is a direction whose components are

$$d_{nj} = \begin{cases} x_{nj}(\Psi_{nj} - \mu c_{nj} - \nu_j) , & \text{if } j \in B , \\ x_{nj}(\Psi_{nj} - \mu c_{nj}) , & \text{if } j \notin B , \end{cases} \tag{115}$$

for problem (70)–(73), and

$$d_{nj} = \begin{cases} x_{nj}(\Psi_{nj} - \mu_n c_{nj} - \nu_j) , & \text{if } j \in B , \\ x_{nj}(\Psi_{nj} - \mu_n c_{nj}) , & \text{if } j \notin B , \end{cases} \tag{116}$$

for problem (74)–(77). The multipliers μ, μ_n, and ν_j are solutions to the following sets of simultaneous linear equations:

$$\sum_{n,j} x_{nj} c_{nj} \Psi_{nj} = \mu \sum_{n,j} c_{nj}^2 x_{nj} + \sum_{\substack{n \\ j \in L}} x_{nj} c_{nj} \nu_j \tag{117}$$

and

$$\sum_n x_{nj} \Psi_{nj} = \mu \sum_n x_{nj} c_{nj} + \nu_j S_j , \qquad j \in L , \tag{118}$$

for problem (70)–(73), and

$$\sum_j x_{nj} c_{nj} \Psi_{nj} = \mu_n \sum_j c_{nj}^2 x_{nj} + \sum_{j \in L} x_{nj} c_{nj} \nu_j , \qquad \forall n , \tag{119}$$

and

$$\sum_n x_{nj} \Psi_{nj} = \sum_n \mu_n c_{nj} x_{nj} + \nu_j S_j , \qquad j \in L , \tag{120}$$

for problem (74)–(77).

It is left as an exercise to the reader to show that d is a feasible convenient direction.

5 Concluding comments on further research

It has been shown how a general mathematical framework can be built which covers a wide range of modelling problems in regional analysis and planning. Some examples have been given where the new theory has been applied to 'old' problems. A first direction for further research could be to use the theory as a guide to the formulation of 'new' problems, or maybe new extensions of old ones. For example, the generalized SIA framework could be used to extend and relax the strict economic-base assumptions. This can result in more disaggregated models and in the possibility of accounting for interaction patterns other than those of the economic base.

A second research direction is obviously that of improvement in computational techniques. Most of the proposed algorithms need numerical testing. Moreover, they need not be the ones best suited to our programming problems, since they were derived from theoretical rather than computational arguments. A promising new issue is that of second-order algorithms, which use information both from first and second derivatives. They may give faster convergence, although at the expense of some additional computational effort for each iteration. Besides, there are reasons to believe that a second-order formulation will also give further insight from the theoretical standpoint.

A third challenging research issue is that of dynamic formulation, which leads to optimal-control problems. We can look to equations (14) as steady-state conditions for the differential equations

$$\frac{\mathrm{d}P_{nj}}{\mathrm{d}t} = \alpha_n \left(Q_{nj} + \sum_m \pi_{mn} \sum_i P_{mi} q_{ij}^m - P_{nj} \right) , \qquad \forall j, n , \tag{121}$$

where the α_n are constant rates and t denotes time. The dynamic analogue of problem (53)–(55) is

$$\text{maximize} \int_0^\infty \exp(-\lambda t)\Psi \, \mathrm{d}t \tag{122}$$

subject to

$$\frac{\mathrm{d}P_{nj}}{\mathrm{d}t} = \alpha_n \left(Q_{nj} + \sum_m \pi_{mn} \sum_i P_{mi} q_{ij}^m - P_{nj} \right) , \qquad \forall j, n , \tag{123}$$

$$\sum_j x_{nj} = 1 , \qquad \forall n , \tag{124}$$

and

$$x_{nj} \geqslant 0 , \qquad \forall j, n , \tag{125}$$

where λ is a discount rate. The Pontryagin conditions (Pontryagin et al, 1962) for this problem can easily be written down, but for a full computational solution there is still some work to be done.

References
Bertuglia C S, Leonardi G, 1978 "Un modello di localizzazione dei servizi a più livelli" *Atti delle Giornate, Associazione Italiana di Ricerca Operativa, Urbino* pp 127-146
Chiang C L, 1968 *Introduction to Stochastic Processes in Biostatistics* (John Wiley, New York)
Coelho J D, Williams H C W L, 1979 "On the design of land use plans through locational surplus maximisation" *Papers of the Regional Science Association* forthcoming (presented at the 17th European Congress of the Regional Science Association, Krakow, Poland)

Coelho J D, Wilson A G, 1976 "The optimum location and size of shopping centres" *Regional Studies* **10** 413-421

Fletcher R, 1970 "A class of methods for nonlinear programming with termination and convergence properties" in *Integer and Nonlinear Programming* Ed. J Abadie (North Holland, Amsterdam) pp 157-175

Fletcher R, 1972 "Minimizing general functions subject to linear constraints" in *Numerical Methods for Non-linear Optimization* Ed. F A Lootsma (Academic Press, New York) pp 279-296

Harris B, 1964 "A model of locational equilibrium for retail trade" Penn-Jersey Transportation Study, Philadelphia, Pa (mimeo)

Harris B, Wilson A G, 1978 "Equilibrium values and dynamics of attractiveness terms for production-constrained spatial-interaction models" *Environment and Planning A* **10** 371-388

Leonardi G, 1973 "Localizzazione ottimale dei servizi urbani" *Ricerca Operativa* **12** 15-43

Leonardi G, 1978 "Optimum facility location by accessibility maximizing" *Environment and Planning A* **10** 1287-1305

Mangasarian O L, 1969 *Nonlinear Programming* (McGraw-Hill, New York)

Pontryagin L S, Boltyanskii V S, Gamkrelidze R V, Mishchenko E F, 1962 *The Mathematical Theory of Optimal Processes* (John Wiley, New York)

Richardson H W, 1969 *Regional Economics* (Praeger, New York)

Wilson A G, 1971 "A family of spatial interaction models, and associated developments" *Environment and Planning* **3** 1-32

Wilson A G, 1977 "Spatial interaction and settlement structure: towards an explicit central place theory" WP-200, School of Geography, University of Leeds, Leeds

Zangwill W I, 1969 *Nonlinear Programming* (Prentice-Hall, Englewood Cliffs, NJ)

A Locational-surplus Maximisation Model of Land-use Plan Design

J D COELHO
University of Lisbon

1 Introduction

The strong development of the modelling approach to land-use-plan design from the start of the sixties has been sustained by two lines of work: one is founded upon optimisation methods and uses linear programming (LP) as the main mathematical tool—it has given rise to considerable modelling experience (Herbert and Stevens, 1960; Schlager, 1965; Ben-Shahar et al, 1969; Farnsworth et al, 1969; Young, 1972; Coelho, 1973; Jenkins and Robson, 1974; Ripper and Varaiya, 1974; and many others); the other, first established by analogy with Newton's law of gravitational attraction between two bodies, is based on a vast family of gravity-type models (such as those due, for example, to Lowry, 1964; Crecine, 1964; Lakshmanan and Hansen, 1965; Goldner and Graybeal, 1965; Wilson, 1969; Cripps and Foot, 1969; Echenique et al, 1969; Batty, 1971; Barras et al, 1971; Barra et al, 1974; Putman, 1977; Mackett, 1977). This latter approach has also been enriched by a statistical rationale grounded in the properties of large numbers, through the concept of entropy maximisation (Wilson, 1967).

A number of merits and shortcomings have been pointed out for both methodologies. For example, the great potentialities provided by mathematical programming for land-use-plan design have been emphasised. In fact this approach provides a suitable means to formulate land-use plans based on objectives set down previously. However, the LP models, which have attracted the attention of planners for a long period, are unable to represent the dispersion underpinning a spatial-interaction pattern. This is so because the number of nonzero variables in the optimal solution cannot exceed the number of constraints. Thus, in the case of spatial interaction between activities, and in a transportation-type LP model, only a few interaction variables are allowed to be nonzero at the optimal solution. This is clearly unrealistic and arises from the fact that spatial interaction is essentially nonlinear. Another limitation of the LP approach is the linear formulation of the objective function, which implies fixed rates of substitution between its elements and therefore "goes completely contrary to a basic premise of economics—the so-called Law of Diminishing Marginal Returns" (Parry-Lewis, 1969). A third limitation concerns the geometry of the feasible-solutions polyhedron, which implies that a small change in data may provoke a substantial change in the optimal solution, caused by a jump from one vertex to another.

With the second methodology, the family of gravity models has proved to be a reasonably satisfactory tool for estimating and forecasting spatial-interaction flows between land-use activities for which no better methods are yet available. It has been emphasised, however, that it is a descriptive rather than explanatory approach. Schneider (1959), for example, has written "the cardinal failure of the gravity model is that it is not explanatory and does not really try to be".

This paper discusses a model formulated for the new town of Santo André, Portugal, based on the maximisation of a nonlinear locational-surplus function which is consistent with the behavioural concepts underpinning the process of location choice (Coelho and Williams, 1977; Coelho, 1977). This model of land-use-plan design has the advantage of a mathematical-programming formulation and ensures simultaneously that the gravity disperson encountered in spatial interaction is generated, and thus brings together the two methodologies described earlier. In addition, when the dispersion parameters tend to infinity and the cost functions are assumed linear, then an LP model is obtained as the limiting case [this is fully consistent with the result of Evans (1973) for the gravity transportation model].

A heavy-industrial and port complex is being constructed in Sines, a few miles to the south of Santo André. It is proposed that the heavy-industrial zone will include a refinery and petrochemical complex, steel and metal industries, a complex for processing of the rich pyrites deposit located in Aljustrel, less than fifty miles from Santo André, which gives rise to several nonferrous metallurgies, and a fertilisers complex. The problem under consideration consists of a comprehensive evaluation of a number of alternative location strategies for the new urban centre (see figures 1 and 2). The model described is a fundamental tool in that evaluation process since it generates the 'optimal' land-use configuration for each alternative location strategy and provides estimates of the overall transportation costs for work and service trips.

In the next section the concepts underpinning the locational-surplus maximisation (LSM) approach for land-use-plan evaluation and design are briefly reviewed. In section 3 the LSM framework is outlined. The planning problems confronted in the new town of Santo André are discussed in section 4, and a model of locational-surplus maximisation for the distribution of residential, employment, and services activities is formulated with regard to the constraints resulting from the planning considerations. Primal and dual versions of the model are provided. The great advantage for numerical computation of the dual representation is emphasised, and it is noted that it determines the primal outcome uniquely through the optimality conditions. Finally a brief evaluation of the empirical work involved in the process of land-use-plan design through the LSM model is offered and some numerical results are presented.

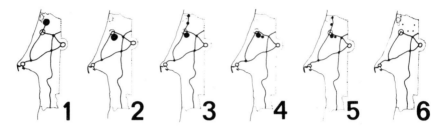

Figure 1. Alternative location strategies (the dots in the north of the area represent optional land-use configurations).

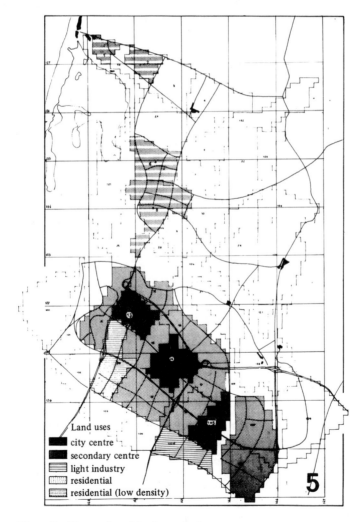

Figure 2. The preferred land-use strategy.

2 Spatial interaction and consumers' surplus

Several authors have pointed out that transportation cost alone is not an appropriate evaluation indicator of (dis)benefit in spatial interaction (Quarmby and Neuberger, 1969; Neuberger, 1971; Williams, 1976; 1977). It has been argued that the Marshallian–Hotelling measure of consumers' surplus (Hotelling, 1938) is, rather, the appropriate criterion. The measure of consumers' surplus was first derived by Neuberger (1971) for singly constrained spatial-interaction models, by direct integration of the demand function. It was later extended by Williams (1976) and Champernowne et al (1976), for a larger class of spatial-interaction models satisfying the Hotelling (1938) integrability conditions, by evoking duality relations established from the mathamatical-programming formulation of those models. These derivations assume implicitly that travel demand is duly represented by the spatial-interaction models and leave out any behavioural considerations regarding the decisionmaking of individuals. In the absence of behavioural grounds, the economic meaning of the users'-benefit measure would be open to controversy. But it turns out, as will be briefly shown, that the same results are obtained in the context of random-utility theory, where each individual is endowed with rational-choice behaviour and the process of location choice is formulated accordingly.

For the purpose of building up a locational-surplus function for land-use-plan evaluation, the derivation of the users'-benefit component associated with a spatial pattern of trips within a random-utility frame of reference shall briefly be outlined. Let us consider population O_i in zone i making a choice between a set of location alternatives, $\{A_j: j = 1, ..., n\}$, at which a given activity may be performed. The net utility or surplus that each individual assigns to the attributes of the alternatives is of course a function of his own tastes, social and cultural habits, and many other factors. Thus a nonuniform valuation of the alternatives will be observed which causes dispersion in the pattern of location choices. Although each individual will ascribe a well-defined net benefit to each alternative, in the population as a whole the surplus will be represented by a 'random' or 'probability' distribution.

McFadden (1974) and Cochrane (1975) have shown that the Weibull distribution,

$$\Phi(s) = \exp[-\alpha \exp(-\beta s)] , \tag{1}$$

where α and β are parameters, is the 'natural' one for describing the random distribution of surplus by virtue of its extremal properties. Now if the random variable s_{ij}, giving the surplus arising to an individual in zone i when location j is chosen, is written as

$$s_{ij} = u_{ij} - c_{ij} + \epsilon_{ij} , \tag{2}$$

where u_{ij} is the fixed component of utility attached to alternative location j by the population of zone i, c_{ij} the cost of selecting that alternative, and

ϵ_{ij} is the random component of utility that simulates the dispersion of preferences, then, if it is assumed that ϵ_{ij} is a Weibull random variable with cumulative distribution function

$$\phi_{ij}(s) = \exp[-w_{ij} \exp(-\beta s)],$$ (3)

where w_{ij} is an attractiveness weight associated with origin i and alternative location j, and β is a dispersion parameter, it is readily shown that the probability, p_{ij}, that alternative j offers the 'greatest surplus' to an individual in zone i is

$$p_{ij} = \frac{w_{ij} \exp[\beta(u_{ij} - c_{ij})]}{\sum_j w_{ij} \exp[\beta(u_{ij} - c_{ij})]} .$$ (4)

Hence the expected number of individuals in zone i who select location j is given by

$$T_{ij} = O_i p_{ij} = A_i O_i w_{ij} \exp[\beta(u_{ij} - c_{ij})]$$ (5)

where

$$A_i = \left\{ \sum_j w_{ij} \exp[\beta(u_{ij} - c_{ij})] \right\}^{-1},$$ (6)

which is a conventional singly constrained spatial-interaction model. It can also be shown that the total expected surplus over the population as a whole is

$$S = \frac{1}{\beta} \sum_i O_i \ln \left\{ \sum_j w_{ij} \exp[\beta(u_{ij} - c_{ij})] \right\} + \text{constant} .$$ (7)

The change in surplus resulting from a change between two situations 1 and 2 is therefore

$$\Delta S = \frac{1}{\beta} \sum_i O_i \ln \left\langle \left\{ \sum_j w_{ij} \exp[\beta(u_{ij} - c_{ij})] \right\}^{(2)} \middle/ \left\{ \sum_j w_{ij} \exp[\beta(u_{ij} - c_{ij})] \right\}^{(1)} \right\rangle$$ (8)

$$= -\frac{1}{\beta} \sum_i O_i \ln \frac{A_i^{(2)}}{A_i^{(1)}} ,$$ (9)

where the superscripts (1) and (2) denote that the quantities within the braces are evaluated for situations 1 and 2 respectively.

On the other hand the singly constrained model (5), (6) can be generated by the mathematical programme (Coelho et al, 1978)

$$\underset{\{T_{ij}\}}{\text{maximise}} \, Z = -\frac{1}{\beta} \sum_{i,j} T_{ij} \left(\ln \frac{T_{ij}}{w_{ij}} - 1 \right) + \sum_{i,j} T_{ij}(u_{ij} - c_{ij})$$ (10)

subject to

$$\sum_j T_{ij} = O_i , \qquad \text{for all } i ,$$ (11)

the dual of which is given by

$$\underset{\{v_i\}}{\text{minimise}} \ V = \frac{1}{\beta} \sum_{i,j} w_{ij} \exp[\beta(u_{ij} - v_i - c_{ij})] + \sum_i v_i O_i \, . \tag{12}$$

The primal and dual variables are related through the optimality conditions

$$T_{ij} = w_{ij} \exp[\beta(u_{ij} - v_i - c_{ij})] \, , \qquad \text{for all } i, j \, , \tag{13}$$

and the balancing factors, A_i, are defined by

$$v_i = -\frac{1}{\beta} \ln O_i A_i \, . \tag{14}$$

Thus the change in surplus (7) is equal to

$$\Delta S = \sum_i O_i [v_i^{(2)} - v_i^{(1)}] \, . \tag{15}$$

By invoking the fact that the first term in equation (12) will be constant at optimality (it is equal to $1/\beta \sum_{i,j} T_{ij}$), we have

$$\Delta S = V^{(2)} - V^{(1)} \, , \tag{16}$$

and, since the optimal primal and dual solutions attain the same value,

$$\Delta S = Z^{(2)} - Z^{(1)} \, . \tag{17}$$

Expression (17) may then be taken as a measure of the users' benefit arising from spatial interaction. These results are extended to a doubly constrained situation by the introduction of shadow prices, γ_j, in equation (7) to accommodate the additional destination constraints; these will represent transfers between the individuals and other individuals or the society in the form of rents or subsidies. Expressions identical to equations (16) and (17) are obtained. A detailed discussion of this can be found in Coelho (1977).

3 Formation of models of locational-surplus maximisation
A general LSM framework for land-use-plan design is (Coelho and Williams, 1977)

maximise S_L = total locational surplus

= users' benefit + producers' surplus , (18)

where S_L denotes locational surplus, subject to
(1) consistency conditions;
(2) economic-base relations;
(3) market-clearing conditions;
(4) planning constraints; and
(5) nonnegativity conditions on planning and interaction variables.
The locational-surplus function associated with a given distribution, A, of, say, activities will typically contain terms that depend on local

coordinates alone, which are usually costs or benefits associated with the configuration of activities in each zone, and terms, embracing the interaction variables, expressing the mutual dependence of land-use activities. Other benefit terms independent of the local coordinates are common to all configurations A and therefore can be dropped out in the process of land-use optimisation.

In order to make the LSM framework more explicit, let us consider the stock and interaction variables which are usually defined in a Lowry-type model:

H_i housing in zone i;

E_j total employment in zone j;

E_j^b basic employment in zone j;

E_j^{sk} service employment in zone j and sector k;

T_{ij} number of work trips from residential zone i to workplace j; and

S_{ij}^k number of service trips from zone i to j for service sector k.

Corresponding notation in bold type will denote the vectors of these variables. A general LSM model may then be formulated as follows:

$$\underset{\{H,\,E^b,\,E^s,\,T,\,S\}}{\text{maximise}}\; S_L = -\frac{1}{\beta^r}\sum_{i,\,j} T_{ij}\left(\ln\frac{T_{ij}}{W_{ij}^r} - 1\right) - \sum_{i,\,j}(u_{ij}^r - c_{ij}^r)T_{ij}$$

$$-\sum_k \frac{1}{\beta^{sk}}\sum_{i,\,j} S_{ij}^k\left(\ln\frac{S_{ij}^k}{W_{ij}^{sk}} - 1\right) - \sum_{i,\,j,\,k}(u_{ij}^{sk} - c_{ij}^{sk})S_{ij}^k$$

$$-\sum_i \int_0^{H_i}\psi_i(t)\,\mathrm{d}t - \sum_{j,\,k}\int_0^{E_j^{sk}}\theta_j^k(t)\,\mathrm{d}t - \sum_j \int_0^{E_j^b}\Omega_j(t)\,\mathrm{d}t \tag{19}$$

subject to

(1) the consistency conditions

$$\sum_j T_{ij} - a^{(1)k}\sum_j S_{ij}^k = 0, \qquad \text{for all } i, k\,; \tag{20}$$

(2) the economic-base relations

$$\sum_i T_{ij} - \sum_k a^{(2)k}\sum_i S_{ij}^k - b^{(2)}E_j^b = 0, \qquad \text{for all } j\,; \tag{21}$$

(3) the market-clearing conditions

$$\sum_j T_{ij} - a^{(3)}H_i = 0, \quad \text{for all } i, \qquad \text{and} \qquad \sum_i S_{ij}^k - a^{(4)k}E_j^{sk} = 0,$$

$$\text{for all } j, k\,; \tag{22}$$

(4) any additional planning constraints; and

(5) the nonnegativity conditions on the planning and interaction variables

$$H \geqslant 0, \qquad E^b \geqslant 0, \qquad E^{sk} \geqslant 0, \quad \text{for all } k, \qquad T \geqslant 0, \qquad S \geqslant 0\,; \tag{23}$$

where the superscripts r and s refer to the residential and service sectors respectively, β^r and β^{sk} are dispersion parameters, $a^{(1)k}$, $a^{(2)k}$, $a^{(3)}$, $a^{(4)k}$, and $b^{(2)}$ are suitably defined coefficients, and ψ_i, θ_j^k, and Ω_j are zone-dependent supply functions in the basic, housing, and service sectors respectively.

Condition (20) expresses that the residential population estimated through the trip matrix, $[T_{ij}]$, is consistent with that estimated from each retail-sector trip matrix $[S_{ij}^k]$. The economic-base condition (21) relates the total employment predicted through $[T_{ij}]$ to the service employment supported by the retail trips, S_{ij}^k, and to the basic-employment component. The market-clearing conditions (22) on the other hand are an expression of the balance between the demand for residential and service activities derived from the work and service trip matrices, $[T_{ij}]$ and $[S_{ij}^k]$, and the supply of housing and service employment by retail sector respectively. Finally, in the objective function (19), the first four terms account for the users' benefit arising from spatial interaction, whereas the remaining three terms are specific producers'-surplus components accompanying the provision of the stock, H, E^{sk}, and E^b. Through the process of maximisation of the users'-benefit terms in S_L, spatial gravity patterns are generated which account for the dispersion of preferences underpinning the population. If the zonal costs of establishing the urban stock, H, E^{sk}, and E^b, are assumed constant and equal to m^h, m^{sk}, and m^b respectively, and if the constant components of utility are transferred to the attractiveness weights, then the S_L function becomes simply

$$S_L = \text{interaction benefits} - \text{establishment costs}$$

$$= -\frac{1}{\beta^r} \sum_{i,j} T_{ij} \left(\ln \frac{T_{ij}}{w_{ij}^r} - 1 \right) - \sum_{i,j} c_{ij}^r T_{ij} - \sum_k \frac{1}{\beta^{sk}} \sum_{i,j} S_{ij}^k \left(\ln \frac{S_{ij}^k}{w_{ij}^{sk}} - 1 \right) - \sum_{i,j,k} c_{ij}^{sk} S_{ij}^k$$

$$- \sum_i m_i^h H_i - \sum_{j,k} m_j^{sk} E_j^{sk} - \sum_j m_j^b E_j^b \ . \tag{24}$$

Since this function is concave, the model that consists of the maximisation of equation (24), subject to constraints (20)–(23), has a unique solution that can be obtained by standard computational methods. This LSM model corresponds to a general supply–demand equilibrium situation, but of course marginal changes in the urban stocks can also be investigated and the appropriate models readily formulated (Coelho and Williams, 1977).

4 A model of locational-surplus maximisation for the new town of Santo André

Now a specific application of the LSM approach to land-use planning for the new town of Santo André will be discussed. The basic aim associated with this modelling application is threefold:
(1) to determine the 'preferred' pattern of residential location;
(2) to design the 'optimal' configuration of employment, including the size of the service centres and the distribution of light industry (the location of heavy industry is an input); and

(3) to generate the spatial-interaction flows consistent with the distribution of residential and employment activities.

A model to generate the optimal urban activity pattern was formulated, based on the criterion of location-surplus maximisation, in accordance with the framework presented. The main specific points of this case study are the following.

1. The service activities are disaggregated into the following sectors: sector 1—service activities associated with city-centre functions; sector 2—service activities associated with secondary-centre functions; and sector 3—recreational activities; these correspond to a classification of the service trips by travel purposes. This division of the service activities has a spatial connotation based on the fact that the service activities associated with each sector are related to particular locations. It also implies a hierarchical structure of the service centres related to the central-place concepts introduced by Christaller (1966). This same type of service-activity disaggregation was adopted by Lowry (1964) in his model of metropolis.

2. The distribution of heavy industry is taken as an input whereas the configuration of light industry is subject to the process of optimisation.

3. Upper bounds on the population of residential zones are given. These bounds coincide with the population of the zone for a number of residential zones with fixed population.

4. Since construction will take place predominantly in urban zones that are roughly homogeneous in terms of topographic and geologic characteristics, it is assumed that the establishment costs which figure in locational-surplus measure (24) are constant and they are therefore omitted from the model.

The following set of zone indices have been defined:

I residential zones;
I_0 residential zones with fixed population;
J employment zones;
J_1 city centre;
J_2 secondary centre;
J_3 recreation zones;
J_4 light-industrial zones;
J_5 heavy-industrial zones.

The LSM model for the new town of Santo André is formulated as follows:

$$\underset{\{T, S, E^{\mathrm{LI}}\}}{\text{maximise}}\, S_{\mathrm{L}} = -\frac{1}{\beta^{\mathrm{r}}} \sum_{\substack{i \in I \\ j \in J}} T_{ij}\left(\ln\frac{T_{ij}}{w_i^{\mathrm{r}}} - 1 - \beta^{\mathrm{r}} c_{ij}^{\mathrm{r}}\right)$$

$$- \sum_{k \in K}\frac{1}{\beta^{sk}} \sum_{\substack{i \in I \\ j \in J_k}} S_{ij}^k\left(\ln\frac{S_{ij}^k}{w_j^{sk}} - 1 - \beta^{sk} c_{ij}^{sk}\right), \qquad (25)$$

where $K = \{1, 2, 3\}$ is the set of service sectors, subject to
(1) the consistency conditions

$$\sum_{j \in J} T_{ij} - a^{(1)k} \sum_{j \in J_k} S_{ij}^k = 0, \qquad \text{for } i \in I, k \in K; \tag{26}$$

(2) the economic-base relations

$$\sum_{i \in I} T_{ij} - \sum_{\substack{k \in K \\ j \in J_k}} a^{(2)k} \sum_{i \in I} S_{ij}^k - \delta^4(j) b^{(2)} E_j^{\text{LI}} = E_j^{\text{HI}}, \qquad \text{for } j \in J, \tag{27}$$

where

$$\delta^4(j) = \begin{cases} 1 & \text{for } j \in J_4, \\ 0 & \text{otherwise}; \end{cases} \tag{28}$$

(3) the density constraint (population bounds)

$$\sum_{j \in J} T_{ij} \begin{cases} < a^{(3)} \overline{P}_i & \text{for } i \in I - I_0, \\ = a^{(3)} \overline{P}_i & \text{for } i \in I_0, \end{cases} \tag{29}$$

where $\overline{P}_i$ is an upper bound on the population of zone i; and
(4) the supply constraint on total light-industrial employment

$$\sum_{\substack{i \in I \\ j \in J_4}} T_{ij} - \sum_{\substack{k \in K \\ j \in J_4}} a^{(2)k} \sum_{i \in I} S_{ij}^k = b^{(2)} E^{\text{LI}} + \sum_{j \in J_4} b^{(2)} E_j^{\text{HI}}; \tag{30}$$

where E^{LI} is the total employment in light industry, E_j^{LI} is the employment in light industry in zone j, E_j^{HI} is the employment in heavy industry in zone j, w_i^{r} and w_j^{sk} are attractiveness weights associated with residential and service-employment location respectively, and all other variables and parameters are defined as previously. In the economic-base relations (27), basic employment has been divided up into light-industrial employment and heavy-industrial employment since the first is subject to the process of optimisation whereas the latter is a model input. The population bounds (29) are self-explanatory, and constraint (30) expresses that the summation of the light-industrial employment over J_4 is the total given employment in light industry.

Associated with this model is the dual programme

$$\underset{\{v, \gamma, \mu, \xi\}}{\text{minimise}} \ U = \frac{1}{\beta^{\text{r}}} \sum_{\substack{i \in I \\ j \in J}} w_i^{\text{r}} \exp\left\{-\beta^{\text{r}}\left[\sum_k v_i^k + \gamma_j + \mu_i + \delta^4(j)\xi + c_{ij}^{\text{r}}\right]\right\}$$

$$+ \sum_{k \in K} \frac{1}{\beta^{sk}} \sum_{\substack{i \in I \\ j \in J_k}} w_j^{sk} \exp\{-\beta^{sk}[a^{(1)k}v_i^k + a^{(2)k}\gamma_j + \delta^4(j)a^{(2)k}\xi - c_{ij}^{sk}]\}$$

$$+ b^{(2)} \sum_{j \in J_s} \gamma_j E_j^{\text{HI}} + b^{(2)}\xi\left(E^{\text{LI}} + \sum_{j \in J_4} E_j^{\text{HI}}\right) + a^{(3)} \sum_{i \in I} \mu_i \overline{P}_i \tag{31}$$

subject to

$$\gamma_j < 0, \quad \text{for } j \in J_4, \qquad \text{and} \qquad \mu_i > 0, \quad \text{for } i \in I - I_0, \tag{32}$$

where ν, γ, μ, and ξ are the dual variables corresponding to constraints (26), (27), (29), and (30) respectively. The conversion from dual to primal variables is established through the optimality conditions

$$T_{ij} = w_i^r \exp\left\{-\beta^r\left[\sum_k \nu_i^k + \gamma_j + \mu_i + \delta^4(j)\xi + c_{ij}^r\right]\right\}, \qquad \text{for } i \in I,\, j \in J,$$

(33)

and

$$S_{ij}^k = w_j^{sk} \exp\{\beta^{sk}[a^{(1)k}\nu_i^k + a^{(2)k}\gamma_j + \delta^4(j)a^{(2)k}\xi - c_{ij}^{sk}]\},$$

$$\text{for } k \in K,\, i \in I,\, j \in J_k, \quad (34)$$

and the set of primal constraints. Conditions (33) and (34) are obtained by equating to zero the partial derivatives with respect to T_{ij} and S_{ij}^k of the Lagrangian function of model (25)–(30).

The dual model is a convex minimisation problem, with bounds on some variables, which has obviously a much smaller size than the primal programme. Relations (33) and (34) are therefore applied for numerical computation of the primal variables from the dual ones. The computational time in the Santo André case study, which has twenty residential and twenty-one employment zones, is around one minute on a Univac 1100/41.

At this stage it is worthwhile to emphasise that this model formulation requires very little data. In fact the data it requires are essentially the same as for the Lowry model. By investigation of a number of industrial-development hypotheses and land-use strategies 1–6 it has been possible to conclude that land-use alternative 4 is the preferred one up to a level of 75 000 inhabitants, at which point it is replaced by land-use alternative 5 (see figure 2), which is obtained from alternative 4 by expanding to the north at a low residential density. The optimal land-use and transportation plan associated with land-use alternative 5 provides yearly savings of 297 million escudos (around 6·5 million dollars) in transportation costs in relation to land-use alternative 1, which was the only one under consideration before this modelling work had started. A comprehensive description of the numerical outcome of the model and the planning recommendations derived from the overall land-use study will be published by the Gabinete da Area de Sines (1979).

5 Conclusion
In this paper it has been attempted to embed the spatial interaction between land-use activities in a framework of social-welfare optimisation, which permits the simultaneous generation of the spatial distribution of activities, and therefore the mathematical-programming and spatial-interaction concepts have been brought together.

The method for the design of land-use and transportation plans discussed here is essentially based on the maximisation of a single objective —the locational-surplus function—which measures economic efficiency, taking into account the benefit arising from accessibility and attractiveness.

The evaluation procedure underpinning the approach is characterised by the framework of cost–benefit analysis, in which the benefits accruing to consumers from accessibility and attractiveness are evaluated in a manner consistent with the basis on which location decisions are taken. But this approach is clearly appropriate for integration into a strategy of multiple-goal evaluation. Also, in order to allow the use of the model as a tool in the process of analysis of alternative land-use patterns, the computer programs may readily be prepared in such a way that any combination of zones for a city centre, secondary centres, and recreational and light-industrial activities may be investigated.

Acknowledgements. I am indebted to Alan Wilson for helpful comments on various stages of this work, but I remain of course solely responsible for any remaining errors. The support of the Junta Nacional de Investigacão Cientifica, Lisbon, is also gratefully acknowledged.

References
Barra T, Echenique M, Guendelman J, Quintana M, 1974 "An urban-regional model" WP-78, Centre for Land Use and Built Form Studies, University of Cambridge, Cambridge
Barras R, Broadbent T A, Cordey-Hayes M, Massey D B, Robinson K, Willis J, 1971 "An operational urban development model of Cheshire" *Environment and Planning* 3 115-234
Batty M, 1971 "Design and construction of a subregional land use model" *Socio-economic Planning Sciences* 5 97-124
Ben-Shahar H, Mazor A, Pines D, 1969 "Town planning and welfare maximisation" *Regional Studies* 3 105-113
Champernowne A F, Williams H C W L, Coelho J D, 1976 "Some comments on urban travel demand analysis, model calibration and the economic evaluation of transport plans" *Journal of Transport Economics and Policy* 10 267-285
Christaller W W, 1966 *Central Places in Southern Germany (Die Zentralen Orte in Süddeutschland)* translated by C W Baskin (Prentice-Hall, Englewood Cliffs, NJ)
Cochrane R A, 1975 "A possible economic basis for the gravity model" *Journal of Transport Economics and Policy* 9 34-49
Coelho J D, 1973 "A location model for the new town of Sines" Gabinete da Area de Sines, Lisbon
Coelho J D, 1977 "The use of mathematical optimisation methods in model based land use planning: an application to the new town of Santo André" Ph D thesis, School of Geography, University of Leeds, Leeds
Coelho J D, Williams H C W L, 1977 "On the design of land use plans through locational surplus maximisation" paper presented at the Seventeenth European Congress, Regional Science Association, Krakow, Poland; forthcoming in *Papers of the Regional Science Association* 40
Coelho J D, Williams H C W L, Wilson A G, 1978 "Entropy maximising submodels within overall mathematical programming frameworks: a correction" *Geographical Analysis* 10(2) 195-201
Crecine J P, 1964 "TOMM (time oriented metropolitan model)" Technical Bulletin 6, Community Renewal Program, Pittsburgh, Pa
Cripps E L, Foot D H S, 1969 "A land-use model for subregional planning" *Regional Studies* 3 243-268

Echenique M, Crowther D, Lindsay W, 1969 "A spatial model of urban stock and activity" *Regional Studies* **3** 281-312

Evans S P, 1973 "A relationship between the gravity model for trip distribution and transportation problems in linear programming" *Transportation Research* **7** 39-61

Farnsworth D, Houghton A G, Pilgrim B, Carter F, 1969 "Systems design project: Macclesfield and district design procedure: progress report" Cheshire County Planning Department, Chester, Cheshire

Gabinete da Area de Sines, 1979 "Estudo das alternativas de desenvolvimento urbano da area de Sines" Gabinete da Area de Sines, Lisbon

Goldner W, Graybeal R S, 1965 "The Bay Area simulation study: pilot model of Santa Clara County and some applications" Centre for Real Estate and Urban Economics, University of California, Berkeley

Herbert J D, Stevens B, 1960 "A model for the distribution of residential activity in urban areas" *Journal of Regional Science* **2** 21-36

Hotelling H, 1938 "The general welfare in relation to taxation and of railway and utility rates" *Econometrica* **6** 242-269

Jenkins P M, Robson A, 1974 "An application of linear programming methodology for regional strategy making" *Regional Studies* **8** 267-279

Lakshmanan T R, Hansen T R, 1965 "A retail market potential model" *Journal of the American Institute of Planners* **31** 134-143

Lowry I S, 1964 "A model of metropolis" RM-4035-RC, The Rand Corporation, Santa Monica, Calif.

Mackett R L, 1977 "A dynamic activity allocation-transportation model" in *Urban Transportation Planning—Current Themes and Future Prospects* Eds P W Bonsall, P J Hills, M Q Dalvi (Abacus Press, Tunbridge Wells, Kent)

McFadden D, 1974 "Conditional logit analysis of qualitative choice behaviour" in *Frontiers in Econometrics* Ed. P Zarembka (Academic Press, New York)

Neuberger H L I, 1971 "User benefit in the evaluation of transport and land use plans" *Journal of Transport Economics and Policy* **5** 52-75

Parry-Lewis J, 1969 "Mis-used techniques in planning: 1. Linear programming" Centre for Urban and Regional Research, University of Manchester, Manchester

Putman S H, 1977 "Calibrating a disaggregated residential allocation model—DRAM" in *London Papers in Regional Science 7. Alternative Frameworks for Analysis* Eds D B Massey, P W J Batey (Pion, London) pp 108-124

Quarmby D A, Neuberger H L I, 1969 "Transport aspects of land use plan evaluation: a note on methodology" Note 140, Mathematical Advisory Unit, Department of the Environment, London

Ripper M, Varaiya P, 1974 "An optimizing model of urban development" *Environment and Planning A* **6** 149-168

Schlager K J, 1965 "A land use plan design model" *Journal of the American Institute of Planners* **31** 103-111

Schneider M, 1959 "Gravity models and trip distribution theory" *Papers and Proceedings of the Regional Science Association* **5** 51-58

Williams H C W L, 1976 "Travel demand models, duality relations and user benefit analysis" *Journal of Regional Science* **16** 147-166

Williams H C W L, 1977 "On the formation of travel demand models and economic evaluation measures of user benefit" *Environment and Planning A* **9** 285-344

Wilson A G, 1967 "A statistical theory of spatial distribution models" *Transportation Research* **1** 253-269

Wilson A G, 1969 "Developments of some elementary residential location models" *Journal of Regional Science* **9** 377-385

Young W, 1972 "Planning—a linear programming model" *Greater London Council Intelligence Unit Quarterly Bulletin* **19** 5-15

A Variable-elasticity-of-substitution Production Function and Urban Land Use: A Theoretical and Empirical Investigation

J B KAU, C F SIRMANS
University of Georgia
C-F LEE
University of Illinois

1 Introduction

In this study the variable-elasticity-of-substitution (VES) production function developed by Revankar (1971a) is used to derive an urban land-use model and to investigate the impact on urban structure of a changing elasticity of substitution of land for capital[1]. Many urban problems such as decentralization, the impact of higher gasoline prices on urban structure, and population growth, cannot be completely understood without knowledge about the elasticity of substitution.

Empirical studies on urban structure have often assumed a fixed value for the elasticity of substitution (σ) between capital and land. Initially urban models assumed very simple types of production functions, such as the fixed-coefficient and linear-coefficient models, with σ equal to zero and infinity respectively. Muth (1969), using a Cobb–Douglas production function with σ equal to unity, derived the conditions for a negative-exponential function between density and distance. Mills (1972a), also using Cobb–Douglas functions, developed additional insights into urban structure. The basic concept of the Mills and Muth models is the trade-off between lower housing prices and greater transportation costs as the commuting distance to the job increases. As various parameters affecting this trade-off change, the urban spatial structure alters shape. Recent criticisms of these models by Wheaton (1977) and Diamond (1978) indicate that more attention must be paid to the impact of amenities and to locational choice. Although realistic urban-location patterns are complex, the Mills and Muth models can be used to understand certain important characteristics of urban areas. Examples would include the benefits and effects of transport improvements such as a rapid-transit system, or the effects of population-density restrictions or large-lot zoning on urban spatial structure.

The value of σ can range between zero and infinity; thus any empirical study using production functions which assumes any specific constant

---

[1] Other forms of VES production functions have been developed (see Bruno, 1968; Liu and Hildebrand, 1965; Sato, 1975). Revankar's VES production function was selected since it is a generalized case of the Cobb–Douglas production function and it also allows us to discriminate between the VES and the CES (constant-elasticity-of-substitution) production functions on statistical grounds.

value of σ can lead to specification bias. (Specification bias means that the impact of changes in the model's parameters, such as income and transportation costs, are incorrectly measured, which could lead to false conclusions.) This study will test whether the Mills and Muth models are incorrectly specified because of their assumption of a fixed elasticity of substitution.

Recently Fallis (1975), Kau and Lee (1976a), and Muth (1975) have used a constant-elasticity-of-substitution (CES) production function to investigate the structure of a city. The CES production function arbitrarily constrains σ to be a constant and does not allow it to vary with a change in the price of land or capital (that is, with changes in the factor-input ratio). However, as demonstrated by Hicks (1948) and Allen (1956), σ can vary depending on the factor combinations and output. Relative factor prices vary over a wide range within an urban area, and result in a variety of capital–land ratios (K/L) whose range is exemplified by the difference between high-rise apartments and single-family dwellings. Thus a CES production function with a constant σ within a specified urban area will lead to specification bias. Revankar's VES production function incorporates the impact of the elasticity of substitution (σ) and the K/L ratio, and thus eliminates any specification bias associated with changes in σ and the factor ratio.

In section 2 the importance of allowing changes in the elasticity of substitution within an urban area is discussed. Also the bias in the density gradient resulting from omitting changes in σ is investigated. In section 3 a density gradient is derived by use of a VES production function incorporating technological change. The bias of the rent gradient and density gradient associated with a Cobb–Douglas production function is explored. In section 4 empirical estimates are presented for the elasticity of substitution associated with CES and VES production functions. It is shown that the VES method can be used to take the change of σ into account. Finally, in section 5, the results of this paper are summarized.

2 Impact of the elasticity of substitution on the density–distance function

The VES production function differs from the CES production function in its isoquant mapping. [An isoquant mapping is a set of curves showing all possible (efficient) combinations of inputs capable of producing a corresponding set of outputs.] The elasticity of substitution (the percent change in the capital–land ratio divided by the percent change in their price ratio) for the CES production function is the same at all points on the isoquant mapping, and is thus independent of output and of the K/L ratio. The VES production function does not require that the elasticity of substitution be the same. Thus σ can vary with output and with changes in the K/L ratio; it can increase steadily from zero to infinity.

In terms of the isoquants, this is demonstrated by their becoming more flattened with increased output. Also it is shown later in this study that the isoquant becomes flatter with a decrease in the K/L ratio for the same output.

The properties of the VES function are especially important for studies of urban structure. First, studies by Kau and Lee (1976c), Mills (1970), and Muth (1969) have demonstrated the existence of a downward sloping land-rent gradient; therefore the K/L ratio will decrease with increasing distance from the urban center[2]. Thus firms producing urban structures will become more capital-intensive near the urban center.

Second, firms producing urban structures may have significantly different production functions relative to output. For example, firms producing high-rise condominiums near the urban center may have significantly different isoquant mappings than firms producing single-family dwellings on the outskirts of an urban area[3].

Third, because of natural and technological limitations, the ability to substitute capital for land decreases with increasing capital intensity. For example, the heights of buildings are limited by space requirements for elevators and the size of the foundation. Therefore the decrease in land rents with distance from the urban center and the corresponding decrease in the K/L ratio results in the elasticity of substitution increasing with distance.

Technological limitations, changing K/L ratios, and different production functions make the Cobb–Douglas and CES production functions inefficient tools for analyzing urban structure. Hence the statistical studies on urban structure which use Cobb–Douglas (Mills, 1972a; Muth, 1969) or CES (Fallis, 1975; Koenker, 1972; Muth, 1975; Tooze, 1976) production functions have biased empirical estimates.

The effect of variation in rentals and in the elasticity of substitution on the intensity of residential land use can be investigated by use of the

---

[2] The relationship estimated by use of data from Ann Arbor, Michigan (see section 4) is

$$\ln\frac{K}{L} = 0 \cdot 247 - 0 \cdot 122 \ln u, \qquad \text{with } \overline{R}^2 = 0 \cdot 75,$$
$$\phantom{\ln\frac{K}{L} = } (0 \cdot 032)\ (0 \cdot 007)$$

where u is the distance from the urban center and the numbers in parentheses are the standard errors. The price of capital (c) relative to the price of land (r) increased with distance, as indicated by

$$\ln\frac{c}{r} = 0 \cdot 969 + 0 \cdot 953 \ln u, \qquad \text{with } \overline{R}^2 = 0 \cdot 82.$$
$$\phantom{\ln\frac{c}{r} = } (0 \cdot 053)\ (0 \cdot 041)$$

$\overline{R}^2$ is the corrected R^2 value, where R^2 is the coefficient of multiple correlation; $\overline{R}^2$ takes account of the loss of degrees of freedom caused by the addition of a variable.
[3] Data in this study are for multifamily dwellings only. Therefore it is assumed for the empirical estimates that the production function is the same for different outputs and firms.

theoretical framework developed by Muth (1969). The essence of the
Muth model necessary for this paper is contained in the derivation of the
locational equilibrium of producers. Producers of housing combine land
and capital in production to maximize profits. Therefore

$$\pi = P(L, K)Q(L, K) - rL - cK , \tag{1}$$

where

π is profit,
P is the price of a unit of housing (dependent on L and K),
Q is the output of housing (dependent on L and K),
L is the input of land,
K is the input of capital,
r is the price of a unit of land, and
c is the price of a unit of capital.

If it is assumed that housing prices and wages vary only with distance,
u, from the central business district (CBD) and that there are similar
production functions for each unique location, differentiation of
equation (1), a rearrangement of terms, and the assumption that in
equilibrium $d\pi = 0$ give

$$\frac{1}{r}\frac{\partial r}{\partial u} = \frac{1}{\rho_L}\left(\frac{1}{P}\frac{\partial P}{\partial u}\right) - \frac{\rho_K}{\rho_L}\left(\frac{1}{c}\frac{\partial c}{\partial u}\right), \tag{2}$$

where

$$R_L = \frac{rL}{PQ} \quad \text{and} \quad R_K = \frac{cK}{PQ} . \tag{3}$$

Equation (2) implies that the rents on land will be bid up by firms in
locations where the product price is high owing to favorable location.

The effects of variation in land rents and in the elasticity of substitution
on land use can be derived by assuming that factor payments exhaust
receipts. Thus

$$PQ = rL + cK . \tag{4}$$

Dividing both sides by L, differentiating with respect to u, using the
definition of the elasticity of substitution and equation (2), and assuming
no variation in capital costs, one derives the following equation:

$$\frac{\partial}{\partial u}\left(\ln\frac{PQ}{L}\right) = \left[1 + \frac{R_K}{R_L}\sigma(u)\right]\frac{1}{P}\frac{\partial P}{\partial u} < 0 . \tag{5}$$

PQ/L is a measure of the intensity of residential land use in terms of the
value of housing produced per unit of land. The negative sign of
equation (5) indicates the slope of the specified density function. The
slope varies inversely with the relative importance of land and directly
with the elasticity of substitution and $\partial P/\partial u$.

The variations in the slope of the curve which relates the logarithm of the value of housing per square mile to distance from the CBD is obtained by differentiating equation (5) with respect to u. It is assumed that σ, the elasticity of substitution, is a function of distance, u. The result is

$$\frac{\partial^2}{\partial u^2}\left(\ln\frac{PQ}{L}\right) = \left[1 + \frac{R_K}{R_L}\sigma(u)\right]\frac{\partial}{\partial u}\left(\frac{1}{P}\frac{\partial P}{\partial u}\right) + \frac{1}{P}\frac{\partial P}{\partial u}\left\{\sigma(u)[\sigma(u) - 1]\frac{R_K}{R_L}\frac{1}{r}\frac{\partial r}{\partial u}\right\}$$
$$+ \frac{1}{P}\frac{\partial P}{\partial u}\frac{R_K}{R_L}\frac{\partial\sigma(u)}{\partial u} . \tag{6}$$

It has been shown by Muth (1969) that the slope of the log price–distance function tends to decline numerically with distance from the CBD. Thus

$$\frac{\partial}{\partial u}\left(\frac{1}{P}\frac{\partial P}{\partial u}\right) \geq 0 . \tag{7}$$

The second term on the right-hand side of equation (6) represents the bias associated with assuming a Cobb–Douglas function. Empirically (demonstrated later in the paper) σ ranges from $0\cdot09$ to $0\cdot93$. The theoretical model indicates that $(\partial P/\partial u)/P \leq 0$ and $\partial r/\partial u \leq 0$. Also R_K/R_L increases with distance[4] when $\sigma < 1$. Thus the second term on the right-hand side of equation (6) is negative or zero.

The third term on the right-hand side of equation (6) represents the bias associated with assuming a constant elasticity of substitution and provides the impact of changing elasticity of substitution on density. Since empirically it will be shown that σ increases with distance and since $\sigma < 1$, R_K/R_L increases with distance. Thus, since $(\partial P/\partial u)/P \leq 0$, the third term on the right-hand side is negative or zero.

The second and third terms both indicate a density function concave to the origin, whereas the first term would produce a convex curve. The negative curvature of the second two terms tends to offset the positive curvature imparted to equation (6) by the log price–distance function. Hence the density gradient may be approximately constant even though the price gradient declines with distance from the CBD. If the impact of variations in the elasticity of substitution is greater than the convexity imposed by the price–distance function then the density gradient may have a negative curvature, so that population densities would decline less rapidly than negative-exponentially with distance from the CBD. In this case, if the price gradient is held constant, an increase in demand for

[4] The total value of capital relative to total land varied with respect to distance according to

$$\ln\frac{cK}{rL} = 1\cdot379 + 0\cdot392\ln u , \qquad \text{with } \overline{R}^2 = 0\cdot42 .$$
$$(0\cdot053)\ (0\cdot042)$$

This is to be expected since the elasticity (σ) is less than one.

housing would increase the output of housing and population more
rapidly in the outer parts of the city.

Urban models using Cobb–Douglas or CES production functions or the
generalized Muth (1969) model, as represented by equations (2) and (5)
and the first two terms on the right-hand side of equation (6), will be
biased in their prediction of structural changes. Transformation procedures
and statistical techniques have been developed by Kau and Lee (1976c;
1977) to reduce the extent of this bias.

The purpose of this section has been to demonstrate the bias associated
with restricting the elasticity of substitution to unity as well as with
assuming a constant elasticity of substitution throughout an urban area.
In the following section the VES production function is used to derive
the density gradient, and the bias of the density gradient derived from the
Cobb–Douglas production function is investigated.

3 The density gradient: a VES approach

A production function which incorporates the impact of changing
elasticities of substitution, capital–land ratios, and technologies is the VES
function presented by Revankar (1971b),

$$H_t(u) = A \exp(zt)[K_t(u)]^{\alpha(1-\delta\rho)}[L_t(u) + (\rho-1)(1+bt)K_t(u)]^{\alpha\delta\rho} , \qquad (8)$$

where

$H_t(u)$	is the output of housing services u miles from the urban center at time t,
$K_t(u)$	is the input of capital u miles from the urban center at time t,
$L_t(u)$	is the input of land u miles from the urban center at time t, and
$A, \lambda, \alpha, \delta, \rho, b$	are parameters such that

$$A > 0, \qquad \alpha > 0, \qquad\qquad\qquad\qquad\qquad\qquad\qquad (9)$$

$$0 < \delta < 1, \qquad 0 \leqslant \delta\rho \leqslant 1, \qquad\qquad\qquad\qquad\qquad (10)$$

and

$$\frac{L_t(u)}{K_t(u)} > \frac{(1-\rho)(1+bt)}{1-\delta\rho} . \qquad\qquad\qquad\qquad\qquad (11)$$

Neutral technical change is represented by $\exp(zt)$, with z referred to as
the neutrality parameter. Nonneutral technical change is reflected by the
term $1 + bt$, which is linear in time, with b referred to as the nonneutrality
parameter.

A neutral technological change does not alter the marginal productivity
ratio, whereas a nonneutral technical change is capital-using (land-using)
if it increases the marginal product of capital (land) relative to land
(capital), while holding the capital–land ratio constant.

The elasticity of substitution for the VES function (8) is

$$\sigma_t = \left[1 + \frac{(\rho - 1)(1 + bt)}{1 - \delta\rho} \right] \frac{K_t(u)}{L_t(u)} . \tag{12}$$

In this formulation σ_t varies linearly with time at each capital–land ratio. The presence of b measures the effect of bias in technical change in terms of its effect on the elasticity of substitution. Also σ_t varies with the capital–land ratio in each time period. Thus, as was astutely demonstrated by Revankar (1971b), the elasticity of substitution has a two-way linear dependence: (1) on t for a given capital–land ratio and (2) on the capital–land ratio for a given t. The VES function reduces to the Cobb–Douglas function when $\rho = 1$, for all t.

A demand function for housing services at u for a given time t, $d_t(u)$, is defined as

$$d_t(u) = Bw_t^{\theta_1} [P_t(u)]^{\theta_2} , \tag{13}$$

where

B is a scale parameter and depends upon the units in which housing services are measured,

w_t is the income for workers for a given time period t,

$P_t(u)$ is the price of housing services at distance u for a given time period t,

θ_1 is income elasticity, and

θ_2 is price elasticity.

From equation (8) the relationships between the value of the marginal product and its rental rates for land and capital, $r_t(u)$ and c_t respectively, can be written as

$$\frac{\partial H_t(u)}{\partial L_t(u)} = \alpha\delta\rho \frac{H_t(u)}{L_t(u) + (\rho - 1)(1 + bt)K_t(u)} = \frac{r_t(u)}{P_t(u)} \tag{14}$$

and

$$\frac{\partial H_t(u)}{\partial K_t(u)} = \alpha(1 - \delta\rho)\frac{H_t(u)}{K_t(u)} + \alpha\delta\rho(\rho - 1)(1 + bt)\frac{H_t(u)}{L_t(u) + (\rho - 1)(1 + bt)K_t(u)}$$

$$= \frac{c_t}{P_t(u)} . \tag{15}$$

From equations (14) and (15) the marginal rate of substitution of capital for land, S_t, is

$$S_t = \frac{(\rho - 1)(1 + bt)}{\delta\rho} + \frac{1 - \delta\rho}{\delta\rho} \frac{L_t(u)}{K_t(u)} . \tag{16}$$

Note that S_t changes linearly with time, and capital intensity remains constant. If the technical bias is capital-using then the time rate of increase in S_t at a fixed capital intensity is

$$\frac{dS_t}{dt} = \frac{(\rho - 1)b}{\delta\rho} > 0 . \tag{17}$$

The time elasticity of S_t is

$$E_t = (\rho - 1)b \bigg/ \left[(\rho - 1)(1 + bt) + (1 - \delta\rho)\frac{L_t(u)}{K_t(u)}\right] . \tag{18}$$

The elasticity is higher at greater capital–land ratios; that is, higher $K_t(u)/L_t(u)$ ratios lead to a greater rate of capital-using inventions.

From equations (14) and (15) we have

$$L_t(u) = \alpha P_t(u)H_t(u)\left[\frac{\delta\rho}{r_t(u)} - \frac{(1 - \delta\rho)(\rho - 1)(1 + bt)}{c_t - r_t(u)(\rho - 1)(1 + bt)}\right] \tag{19}$$

and

$$K_t(u) = P_t(u)H_t(u)\frac{\alpha(1 - \delta\rho)}{c_t - r_t(u)(\rho - 1)(1 + bt)} . \tag{20}$$

As $\alpha = 1$, substituting equations (19) and (20) into equation (8) we have

$$P_t(u) = A^{-1}\exp(-zt)[c_t - r_t(u)(\rho - 1)(1 + bt)]^{1 - \delta\rho}(1 - \delta\rho)^{\delta\rho - 1}$$
$$\times [r_t(u)]^{\delta\rho}(\delta\rho)^{-\delta\rho} . \tag{21}$$

From equation (21) the price elasticities of housing with respect to c and $r(u)$ can be rewritten as

$$\frac{\partial P_t(u)}{\partial c_t}\frac{c_t}{P_t(u)} = \frac{c_t(1 - \delta\rho)}{c_t - r_t(u)(\rho - 1)(1 + bt)} \tag{22}$$

and

$$\frac{\partial P_t(u)}{\partial r_t(u)}\frac{r_t(u)}{P_t(u)} = \frac{\delta\rho c_t - r_t(\rho - 1)(1 + bt)}{c_t - r_t(\rho - 1)(1 + bt)} . \tag{23}$$

Equations (22) and (23) allow the elasticities of housing services with respect to c_t and $r_t(u)$ to vary with changes in c_t and $r_t(u)$. These elasticities will reduce to $1 - \alpha$ and α respectively when the elasticity of substitution between land and capital is unity. This is the case obtained with the Cobb–Douglas function.

Muth (1969), using constrained utility maximization, has derived a differential equation to describe the relationship between the change in the cost of housing and the change in commuting cost as

$$P'_t(u)d_t(u) + T = 0 , \tag{24}$$

where
$P'_t(u)$ is the slope of $P_t(u)$ and
T is the cost of commuting.

Substituting equation (13) into equation (24) we have

$$P_t'(u)Bw_t^{\theta_1}[P_t(u)]^{\theta_2} + T = 0. \tag{25}$$

By use of the initial condition of equation (25), obtained from equation (24), the solution of the differential equation (25) can be written as

$$P_t(u) = \left[\bar{P}_t^{\theta_2+1} + \frac{T(\bar{u}-u)(\theta_2+1)}{Bw_t^{\theta_1}} \right]^{1/(\theta_2+1)}, \tag{26}$$

where
$\bar{u}$ is the distance from the city center to the edge of the urban area, and

$$\bar{P}_t = P_t(\bar{u}). \tag{27}$$

Substituting equation (21) into equation (26) we have

$$\left[\bar{P}_t^{\theta_2+1} + \frac{T(\bar{u}-u)(\theta_2+1)}{Bw_t^{\theta_1}} \right]^{1/(1+\theta_2)}$$
$$= A^{-1}\exp(-zt)[c_t - r_t(u)(\rho-1)(1+bt)]^{1-\delta\rho}(1-\delta\rho)^{\delta\rho-1}[r_t(u)]^{\delta\rho}(\delta\rho)^{-\delta\rho} \tag{28}$$

Equation (28) can be rewritten as

$$r_t(u) = [A\exp(zt)(\delta\rho)^{\delta\rho}(1-\delta\rho)^{1-\delta\rho}]^{1/\delta\rho}c_t^{(\delta\rho-1)/\delta\rho}$$
$$\times \left[1 - \frac{r_t(u)}{c_t}(\rho-1)(1+bt) \right]^{(\delta\rho-1)/\delta\rho} \left[\bar{P}_t^{\theta_2+1} + \frac{T(\bar{u}-u)(\theta_2+1)}{Bw_t^{\theta_1}} \right]^{1/\delta\rho(\theta_2+1)} \tag{29}$$

This implies that the explicit relationship between $r_t(u)$ and u cannot be derived unless ρ is equal to unity. If $\rho = 1$ then equation (29) reduces to

$$r_t(u) = [A\exp(zt)\delta^{\delta}(1-\delta)^{1-\delta}]^{1/\delta}c_t^{(\delta-1)/\delta}$$
$$\times \left[\bar{P}_t^{\theta_2+1} + \frac{T(\bar{u}-u)(\theta_2+1)}{Bw_t^{\theta_1}} \right]^{1/\delta(\theta_2+1)}, \tag{30}$$

where

$$\bar{P}_t = A^{-1}\exp(-zt)(1-\delta)^{\delta-1}\delta^{-\delta}\bar{r}_t^{\delta}c_t^{1-\delta} \tag{31}$$

and

$$\bar{r}_t = r_t(\bar{u}). \tag{32}$$

This is identical to the general case presented by Mills (1972a) except for the time variable.

To derive the relationship between the population density and the rental of land, $r_t(u)$, Mills (1972b, page 84) has defined

$$N_t(u) = \frac{H_t(u)}{d_t(u)}, \tag{33}$$

where

$N_t(u)$ is the number of workers living u miles from the urban center at time t,

$H_t(u)$ is the output of housing services u miles from the urban center at time t, and

$d_t(u)$ is the housing demand per worker living u miles from the urban center at time t.

From equations (19) and (20) it can be shown that

$$K_t(u) = \left\{ \frac{1-\delta\rho}{c_t - r_t(u)(\rho-1)(1+bt)} \Bigg/ \left[\frac{\delta\rho}{r_t(u)} - \frac{(1-\delta\rho)(\rho-1)(1+bt)}{c_t - r_t(u)(\rho-1)(1+bt)} \right] \right\} L_t(u) . \tag{34}$$

Substitution of equation (34) into equation (8) gives

$$H_t(u) = A \exp(zt) L_t(u) \left[\frac{\delta\rho}{r_t(u)} - \frac{(\rho-1)(1-\delta\rho)}{c_t - r_t(u)(\rho-1)(1+bt)} \right]^{-1}$$

$$\times \left[\frac{1-\delta\rho}{c_t - r_t(u)(\rho-1)(1+bt)} \right]^{1-\delta\rho} \left[\frac{\delta\rho}{r_t(u)} \right]^{\delta\rho} . \tag{35}$$

From equations (13) and (21),

$$d_t(u) = B w^{\theta_1} A^{-\theta_2} \exp(-z\theta_2 t) [c_t - r_t(u)(\rho-1)(1+bt)]^{\theta_2(1-\delta\rho)}$$

$$\times (1-\delta\rho)^{\theta_2(\delta\rho-1)} [r_t(u)]^{\delta\rho\theta_2} (\delta\rho)^{-\delta\rho\theta_2} . \tag{36}$$

Substitution of equations (35) and (36) into equation (33) gives

$$D_t(u) = \frac{N_t(u)}{L_t(u)} = B^{-1} w_t^{-\theta_1} A^{\theta_2+1} \exp[zt(\theta_2+1)]$$

$$\times [c_t - r_t(u)(\rho-1)(1+bt)]^{(\theta_2+1)(\delta\rho-1)} (1-\delta\rho)^{(\theta_2+1)(1-\delta\rho)}$$

$$\times \left[\frac{\delta\rho}{r_t(u)} - \frac{(\rho-1)(1-\delta\rho)}{c_t - r_t(u)(\rho-1)(1+bt)} \right]^{-1}$$

$$\times \left[\frac{\delta\rho}{r_t(u)} \right]^{\delta\rho} [r_t(u)]^{-\delta\rho\theta_2} (\delta\rho)^{\delta\rho\theta_2} . \tag{37}$$

This is the population density in terms of c_t, $r_t(u)$, b, t and other parameters.

To compare this density function with those derived from the Cobb–Douglas production function, a static population-density model is derived from equation (37) by removing the time variable. With time removed and $\rho = 1$, then equation (37) reduces to Mills's (1972b) generalized results. If ρ is not equal to zero then c and $r(u)$ are additional variables needed to explain the change of population density within a city. This essentially is due to the VES production function having explicitly taken the K/L ratio into account. The argument can be shown explicitly by rewriting the static version of the VES function as

$$H(u) = A[K(u)]^{\alpha(1-\delta\rho)}[L(u)]^{\alpha\delta\rho}\left[1+(\rho-1)\frac{K(u)}{L(u)}\right]^{\alpha\delta\rho} \tag{38}$$

within a city. The K/L ratio changes over distance, and therefore K/L becomes an important factor in explaining the supply of housing services unless the value of $1-\rho$ is trivial. In sum, the density gradient estimated by using the negative-exponential function is generally biased.

In the following section a regression model (for a particular point in time) is derived for estimating the elasticity of substitution. Some empirical results are estimated to demonstrate the importance of the possible impact of changes in σ on the density gradient.

4 Empirical estimates of the VES function
The VES and CES production functions relate the output–capital ratio to factor prices. The major difference lies in the fact that the VES function is linear and the CES log-linear. If constant returns to scale are assumed, a stochastic model of the VES function may be written (Revankar, 1971a) as:

$$\ln H = b_0 + b_1 X^* + \epsilon_1 , \tag{39}$$

where

$$X^* = (1-\delta\rho)\ln K + \delta\rho \ln[L+(\rho-1)K] , \tag{40}$$

$$b_0 = \ln A , \tag{41}$$

and

$$b_1 = \alpha ; \tag{42}$$

and

$$\frac{H}{K} = F_1 c + F_2 r + \epsilon_2 , \tag{43}$$

where

$$F_1 = \frac{1}{q(1-\delta\rho)} , \tag{44}$$

$$F_2 = \frac{1-\rho}{q(1-\delta\rho)} \tag{45}$$

$$q = \exp\frac{\sigma}{2} , \tag{46}$$

c is the price per unit of capital, and
r is the price per unit of land;

and

$$\frac{L}{K} = G_0 + G_1 \frac{n}{r} + \epsilon_3 ,\tag{47}$$

where

$$G_0 = \frac{1-\rho}{1-\delta\rho}\tag{48}$$

and

$$G_1 = \frac{\delta\rho}{1-\delta\rho} .\tag{49}$$

Thus the estimation of the VES function results in the empirical determination of the parameters γ, α, δ, and ρ. These parameters are estimated by use of Zellner's (1962) seemingly unrelated regression (SUR) technique. The simultaneous estimation of equations (43) and (47) results in efficient estimates for F_1, F_2, G_0, and G_1. With these estimates, ρ and δ can be determined from

$$\rho = 1 - \frac{G_0}{1+G_1} ,\tag{50}$$

and

$$\delta = \frac{G_1}{1+G_1-G_0} .\tag{51}$$

These estimates can in turn be used to estimate equation (39).

The elasticity of substitution, σ, is obtained from

$$\sigma = 1 + \frac{\rho-1}{1-\delta\rho}\frac{K}{L} = 1 - G_0\left(\frac{K}{L}\right).\tag{52}$$

The VES and CES functions are generalizations of the Cobb–Douglas function. Thus a test is necessary to determine the relevance of using a VES or CES function. The relationship between the VES and Cobb–Douglas functions can be tested by use of equation (52) with $G_0 \neq 0$— the elasticity of substitution is thus not equal to one, as implied by the Cobb–Douglas specification. This same test is provided for in the CES function by testing if the slope coefficient is equal to unity in equations (59) and (62).

The data used in this paper, from Koenker (1972), is based on the tax-assessment records for all private multifamily housing constructed in Ann Arbor, Michigan, from 1964 through 1966. The sample consisted of 122 observations. It was assumed that there is no systematic bias in the assessment estimates of actual market values of the properties and the sites. The prices of land and capital were determined as the prices per square foot. The size of the building site and the number of units were contained in the data set.

The seemingly unrelated regression estimates of equations (43) and (47) are (with standard errors in parentheses)

$$\frac{H}{K} = 0.717 + 0.678c + 1.023r \tag{53}$$
$$(0.144) \quad (0.032) \quad (0.011)$$

and

$$\frac{L}{K} = 0.681 + 0.086\frac{c}{r} . \tag{54}$$
$$(0.098) \quad (0.008)$$

Thus

$$\rho = 1 - \frac{G_0}{1 + G_1} = 0.373 \tag{55}$$

and, at the mean K/L ratio,

$$\sigma = 1 - G_0\left(\frac{K}{L}\right) = 0.514 . \tag{56}$$

The capital–land ratio in the sample ranged from 1.336 to 0.104. Thus the elasticity of substitution, derived from equation (53), varies from 0.090 to 0.929. These empirical results tend to support the use of a VES function and lend significant insight into the range of the elasticity of substitution in an urban area.

The factor intensity parameter, δ, is equal to

$$\delta = \frac{G_1}{1 + G_1 - G_0} = 0.212 . \tag{57}$$

The estimate of the production function in equation (39), without restricting the returns-to-scale parameter, α, to unity, is

$$\ln H = 0.270 + 0.930X^* , \qquad \text{with } \overline{R}^2 = 0.962 . \tag{58}$$
$$(0.176) \quad (0.017)$$

Hence $\ln A = 0.270$ and $\alpha = 0.930$.

The marginal conditions for the CES production function are:

$$\ln \frac{H}{K} = F_1' + F_2' \ln c , \tag{59}$$

where

$$F_1' = -\frac{\rho}{1-\rho}\ln\delta - \frac{1}{1-\rho}\ln(1-\delta) \tag{60}$$

and

$$F_2' = \frac{1}{1-\rho} = \sigma ; \tag{61}$$

and

$$\ln\frac{L}{K} = G_0' + G_1' \ln\frac{c}{r} ,$$

(62)

where

$$G_0' = \frac{1}{1-\rho}\ln\frac{\delta}{1-\delta}$$

(63)

and

$$G_1' = \frac{1}{1-\rho} = \sigma .$$

(64)

Equations (59) and (62) were estimated with Zellner's efficient technique by restricting $F_2' = G_1' = \sigma$. These results are (with standard errors in parentheses)

$$\ln\frac{H}{K} = 1\cdot148 + 0\cdot619\ln c$$
$$\quad\quad (0\cdot066)\;\;(0\cdot026)$$

(65)

and

$$\ln\frac{L}{K} = -0\cdot925 + 0\cdot619\ln\frac{c}{r} .$$
$$\quad\quad (0\cdot053)\;\;(0\cdot026)$$

(66)

Thus the elasticity of substitution is $0\cdot619$ in the CES case.

5 Summary and concluding remarks
Based upon the VES production function, a land-use model has been derived to show that neither the Cobb–Douglas nor the CES production functions can take into account a changing elasticity of substitution of capital for land. It has also been shown that the ratio between the rental rates of land and capital may be an additional exploratory variable for the density-gradient function.

The empirical results demonstrate that the VES production function rather than the Cobb–Douglas or the CES production functions should be used to investigate urban land use. To discriminate the CES production function from the VES production function, Lovell (1970) has employed Zarembka's (1968) functional-form approach to test the estimated function-form parameter (λ) for the relation between factor proportions and the factor price ratio. Following Lovell's approach, we have found that $\lambda = 0\cdot6$ for our case. By use of the χ^2 test it is found that λ is significantly different both from one and zero at the 5% significance level. However, at the 1% significance level it is found that λ is significantly different for zero and not significantly different for one. This result tends to support the VES function.

The results indicate that the elasticity of substitution does change with distance in an urban area and that the use of a Cobb–Douglas or CES production function to derive a density gradient will result in biased estimates. A VES production function produces a density-gradient function which decreases at a numerically faster rate with distance. In sum, this study has not only found a most useful application for the VES production function but has also shown that city planning (or urban-structure determination) cannot entirely rely upon the distance variable. The evidence suggests that other parameters may play an important part in determining urban spatial structure. The variation of the elasticity of substitution indicates that institutional or technological constraints exist and that these constraints effect the variation of population density with distance. The results confirm previous evidence by Kau and Lee (1976b) that the capital–land ratio can be taken as a proxy for measuring the impact of technological change and the effect of past development on future land use.

Acknowledgements. Appreciation is extended to Roger Koenker for making his data available and to Roger Lowry of Pion Limited for his useful comments.

References
Allen R G D, 1956 *Mathematical Analysis for Economists* (Macmillan, London)
Bruno M, 1968 "Estimation of factor contribution to growth under structural disequilibrium" *International Economic Review* **9** 49-62
Diamond D Jr, 1978 "Income and residential location in urban areas" Ph D dissertation, Department of Economics, University of Chicago, Chicago, Ill.
Fallis G, 1975 "The technology of production and the location of employment in urban areas" Ph D dissertation, Department of Economics, Princeton University, Princeton, NJ
Hicks J R, 1948 *The Theory of Wages* (P Smith, New York)
Kau J B, Lee C-F, 1976a "Capital–land substitution and urban land use" *Journal of Regional Science* **16** 83-92
Kau J B, Lee C-F, 1976b "Functional form, density gradient and the price elasticity of demand for housing" *Urban Studies* **13** 193-200
Kau J B, Lee C-F, 1976c "The functional form in estimating the density gradient: an empirical investigation" *Journal of the American Statistical Association* **71** 326-327
Kau J B, Lee C-F, 1977 "A random coefficient model to estimate a stochastic density gradient" *Regional Science and Urban Economics* **7** 169-177
Koenker R, 1972 "An empirical note on the elasticity of substitution between land and capital in a monocentric housing market" *Journal of Regional Science* **12** 299-305
Liu T C, Hildebrand G H, 1965 *Manufacturing Production Functions in the United States, 1957* (Cornell University Press, Ithaca, NY)
Lovell C A, 1970 "CES and VES production functions in a cross-section context" *Journal of Political Economy* **4** 705-720
Mills E S, 1970 "Urban density functions" *Urban Studies* **7** 5-20
Mills E S, 1972a *Studies in the Structure of the Urban Economy* (Johns Hopkins University Press, Baltimore, Md)
Mills E S, 1972b *Urban Economics* (Scott Foresman, Glenview, Ill.)

Muth R, 1969 *Cities and Housing* (University of Chicago Press, Chicago, Ill.)

Muth R, 1975 "Numerical solution of urban residential land-use models" *Journal of Urban Economics* **2** 307-332

Revankar N S, 1971a "A class of variable elasticity of substitution production functions" *Econometrica* **39** 60-71

Revankar N S, 1971b "Capital-labor substitution, technological change and economic growth: the U.S. experience, 1929-1953" *Metroeconomica* **23** 154-174

Sato K, 1975 *Production Functions and Aggregation* (North-Holland, Amsterdam: American Elsevier, New York)

Tooze MJ, 1976 "Regional elasticities of substitution in the United Kingdom in 1968" *Urban Studies* **13** 35-44

Wheaton W C, 1977 "Income and urban residence: an analysis of consumer demand for location" *American Economic Review* **67** 620-631

Zarembka P, 1968 "Functional form in the demand for money" *Journal of the American Statistical Association* **63** 502-511

Zellner A, 1962 "An efficient method of estimating seemingly unrelated regressions and tests for aggregation bias" *Journal of the American Statistical Association* **57** 348-368

Quantification of Gains in Manufacturing Imports of Interregional Cooperation among Developing Countries

P N MATHUR
University College of Wales
S R HASHIM
The Maharaja Sayajinas University of Baroda, India

Before the Second World War, the present developing countries were primarily the suppliers of raw materials, whereas the developed countries were the suppliers of manufactured goods. However in the 1950s the share in world manufacture of these developing countries increased to almost 10%. In the 1960s and 1970s there has been no noticeable increase in this share. It seems as if the pattern of production and trade has achieved a new postwar equilibrium in the allocation of manufactures between the developing and the developed world. A new relationship seems to have developed which allocates about 10% of manufacturing activity to the developing world. The hope that this percentage will steadily increase has not been realised.

This implies that in the division of labour some particular types of manufacturing activity have been allocated to the developing countries. Owing to complementarity, the rate of growth of developing countries now seems to be largely determined by the rate of growth of the developed world. Their manufacturing, mining, and agricultural activities seem to be determined exogenously by the developed countries. As developed countries are facing a continuous slowdown of their growth rates, the outlook for the fast economic growth of the developing world seems to be bleak indeed, until and unless the international community decides to give a new thrust by means of restructuring the world economic order. There are two ways in which such a restructuring has been attempted in the past. The first way is trying to increase the penetration of commodities from developing countries into the markets of developed countries. The protracted trade negotiations with the EEC is an example of an attempt in that direction. It is considered that by increasing their share in this market the developing countries would be able to achieve a higher rate of growth than otherwise. However, the experience of the last two decades is hardly encouraging. Most of the developing countries no sooner start showing capabilities of rudimentary manufacturing production than they begin to be discriminated against in the markets of the developed world. The exclusion of Asian ex-colonies of the European nations from the preferential arrangements afforded by the EEC to its African ex-colonies is a strong pointer in this direction. This is understandable, however, as it implies nonefficient jobs being transferred from developed countries to developing countries, which by its very nature cannot be welcome when there is large unemployment in developed countries also.

The second type of action which developing countries have been planning is that of mutual cooperation, so that they can themselves progressively provide a market for the manufacturing goods of each other. Pursuing this line, the developing countries agreed in Lima on a plan of action for industrial development and cooperation, and set a target that by the year 2000 the developing countries should account for at least 25% of the world's manufacturing production. This was reaffirmed by a conference on economic cooperation among developing countries held in Mexico in September 1976. As it is obvious that this goal can not be achieved under the present rules of the game, the Mexican conference declared "Collective self-reliance as a means for the achievement of the fundamental objectives". Its main vehicle has been declared to be "fostering of economic co-operation among themselves, aimed at reinforcing their political and economic independence and their collective work strength in fulfilment of the objectives of the new international economic order".

The question remains, however, as to how useful this approach will be. To what extent will this cooperation really help in industrialisation of the developing world? The problem is of quantifying the gains of cooperation in manufacturing output. Without this, we do not know how much can be achieved by this approach and whether it can be used to achieve the aim. Economic cooperation is a means of providing a larger unified market for various products. This allows not only freer competition among different manufacturers and thus a rise in efficiency, but also allows a free play of that engine of growth on which Adam Smith relied so much, namely the division of labour. But the problem of quantifying the effects of economic cooperation has defied a solution. An attempt has now been made, however, to extend Chenery's (1960) method for assessing such effects. This will help us to get a dimension of the problem rather than a close estimate.

Chenery and his colleagues have shown that on average the per capita imports of manufactures are dependent on per capita income and the population of the country. To estimate the country's imports of manufactures a regression of these on per capita income and population has been undertaken. As we do not know at what rate developing countries will grow up to the year 2000, this exercise was carried out for alternative projected rates of growth. The rates chosen for this exercise were all higher than those experienced in recent past, in the hope that cooperation would enable these countries to plan for higher growth rates. In view of past experience and obvious potentialities, the smallest growth rate was chosen for Asia, larger rates for Africa and Latin America, and the largest rate for the Middle East.

The research division of UNCTAD has repeated the Chenery calculations on the basis of 1970 data for a sample comprising eighty-five developed and developing countries (UNCTAD, 1976). They found that the elasticity of manufacturing imports with respect to income was $1 \cdot 06$ only, whereas that with respect to population was $-0 \cdot 343$. These elasticities show that increasing per capita income does not change the import dependence of a country. The reasons for this inverse relationship between the size of per capita imports and the size of population seem obvious when it is remembered that the larger population implies a larger market. And a larger market not only leads to the increase in the efficiency of production by increasing potential competition, but also allows the production of quite a few new lines which could not survive in a smaller market and would have to be imported. Thus the regression results confirm our prior expectation.

They also give us a tool for deriving an estimate of imported manufactures for a group of countries joined in an economic and monetary union, because in that case the union can be treated as one market. Obviously, these imports will be much less than the total of imports of individual countries in the case where no special effort at cooperation exists. If all these imports were to come from developed countries, the difference between the estimated imports on the assumption of one market, and that on the assumption of many markets, would give an indication of the reduction of dependence of the developing countries on the developed world. However, there are some imports from other developing countries even now for which an adjustment will have to be made in estimating these gains.

As an illustration, suppose that there are two countries of equal size, which are importing 20% of their manufactured goods in their final demand, and all from a third country. If they join together in a common market, their imports do not remain 20%, as above, but become only about 16%. The difference between these two, 4%, is the amount of extra manufactures that will be produced within the countries now, because the size of the market has increased. This implies that now it will become profitable for firms to build plants for simple manufactures which can supply this increased market. Thus economic union will be an effective way of increasing the proportion of manufacturing in these countries.

Empirical articulation of the gains from grouping
To get an idea of the dimensions of the gains from the grouping, the following exercise was carried out. All the developing countries were grouped into twenty-three subgroups, then they were further combined into twelve groups, and these twelve groups were aggregated into four regions of continental size. The four largest groups were those of Asia, the Middle East, Africa, and Latin America. Six different sets of annual growth rates for the developing countries of these four continents were

used for simulation. On the assumption that these growth rates could be achieved between 1973 (base year for the data) and the year 2000, estimates were made for total imports of manufacturing goods on the assumption of different groupings.

As per capita income does not seem to affect per capita imports, different growth rates are immaterial to gains in imports through cooperation. All different growth-rate alternatives give similar results in percentage terms, and these are consolidated in table 1. Column (1) of this table gives the twenty-three groups; each of these groups consists of a number of countries. Column (2) gives the intragroup trade in manufacturing between countries for each group in terms of percentage of

Table 1. Hierarchies of grouping for simulation and estimated intragroup trade as percentage of total trade.

Basic grouping of developing countries (1)	Trade for basic grouping (2)	Trade between basic groupings (3)	Trade within twelve regions (4)	Trade among four regions (5)	Trade with developed world (6)
Continental South-east Asia	0·04	0·27	1·26	18·71	22·17
Asia	2·56				
East South Asia	0·83	1·81			
West South Asia	1·47				
Fertile Crescent	0·91	1·72	3·10		
Arabian Sea Middle East	4·76				
Mediterranean Middle East	2·34	2·50			
African Middle East	6·69				
Ex-French Central Africa	0·10	0·15	1·34		
Central Africa	0·07				
West Africa	0·75	0·49			
Niger and Nigeria	0·12				
Ethiopia	0	0·17			
East Africa	0·48				
Interior South Africa	0·08	0·18			
Coastal South Africa	0·09				
South American High Plateau	1·31	0·49	9·26		
Coastal West South America	0·27				
Mexico	0	1·04			
Other Central America	0·88				
Brazil and Venezuela	2·61	8·18			
Argentina	0				
Caribbean	0·79	0			
Total	27·15	17·02	14·96	18·71	22·17

total estimated imports from developed countries, on the assumption that each of the twenty-three groups acts as a single economic unit. Further, if these twenty-three groups are aggregated into twelve groups, and each of these twelve groups is considered as if it is one common market economy, then the additional intrasubgroup trade within each of these twelve regions is given in column (3), in similar percentage terms. Thus, the estimate of the increment of intragroup trade given in column (2) plus the increment of intragroup trade given in column (3), gives the total intragroup trade for the twelve regions.

A similar exercise is carried out in column (4) for intraregional trade if it is assumed that the twelve regions can unite themselves into four markets. If the whole developing world becomes one huge common market, then the estimate of the extra trade generated among them is that given in column (5). The estimate of the imports of the goods of manufacturing industries from the developed world, in that case, is given in column (6). It may be surmised that if no regional understandings are reached the imports will be almost entirely from developed countries. If on the other hand, only four continental groupings come about without an overall understanding, then the imports from the developed world would be of the order of 41% of the total imports of manufacturing goods. However, if there are two hierarchies of grouping, one of all developing countries and a subgrouping at continental level, the trade with developed countries will be only 22% and 19% will be trade between these four common markets.

Further, if there are only twelve groupings, and each of these groups imports manufactured goods from the developed world only, the extra imports from the developed countries would be of the order of 15% thereby making the total imports from the developed countries about 55% of what they would have been in the absence of common markets. A similar interpretation should be put on the other two figures in the last row of the table.

Conclusions and economic implications

We have seen above that the growth of developed countries has slowed down over the last decade, and in future it is likely to be rather low. This may be partly due to the fact that these developed countries have already reached a productivity level that is constrained by the limits of technological progress. However, developing countries have to do a lot of catching up, and therefore, naturally, they require a much higher rate of growth. With a higher rate of growth their demand for manufactured imports also increases *pari passu*. We have seen that this demand does not decrease in percentage terms with increasing per capita income, and, if the demand is to be met from the output of the developed countries only, the developed countries' imports from the developing world should increase at the same rate as their growth. Otherwise the developing countries will not have the wherewithal to pay for the imports. The unilateral transfer of resources which is called 'foreign aid' is only a temporary palliative, and is very small compared to the total need of foreign resources for this purpose. Further, the commodities that are imported by the developed countries have themselves, by and large, a low income elasticity. This further aggravates the problem of resources for the developing countries. Even if the overall elasticity was equal to one, the developing countries would not be able to grow at a higher rate than the developed ones. When the elasticity is lower than one, this rate may become very low indeed.

We have seen that if all the developing countries could be grouped as one common market, the necessity of manufacturing imports reduces to the level of about one-fifth of what it would have been otherwise. This would imply that this particular 'bottle neck' for growth of the developing countries gets very much reduced. In fact, if there were no other impediments to their growth, this would imply growth five-fold that which would be possible otherwise. At that level other constraints to growth might occur. Probably we need to loosen this impediment to growth by only 50%, rather than the 80% that seems to be possible. If we require only 50% loosening, this can be achieved in two ways. First, we may try to have twelve common markets of the developing world similar to the twelve groupings that we have made above, and assume that each common market in itself will purchase its imports from developed countries only to the extent that they do now. Or, second, a big common market for the developing world may be envisaged which is much more flexible than the assumption of one country-like economy would allow. Thus, it may be so relaxed in its import policy that instead of allowing only 20% of imports to come from nonmarket economies, it might allow more than double the amount. I think a common-market understanding, where there is a strictness of import controls for the purpose of individuals, which is relaxed for the purpose of government or some other variant of the same, may prove to be of this type. This may be more easily attainable than a very strict common-market import-control policy.

Thus we have a method for establishing the dimensions of inter-constituent, intracommon-market trade in manufacturing countries in case several developing countries decide to join into an economic common market. To get a more complete picture, this information may be supplemented by the estimates for trade in agricultural and mineral products. As these commodities are more specific in identification and in marketing and trading arrangements, it is much easier to make a detailed trading model for them from the theoretical as well as from the data point of view. This can be determined by adding a linear-programming model to these on the lines described previously by the author (see Hashim and Mathur, 1975; Mathur, 1976).

References

Chenery H B, 1960 "Patterns of industrial growth" *American Economic Review* **50** (September) 624–654

Hashim S R, Mathur P N, 1975 "Interregional programming models for economic development" in *London Papers in Regional Science 5. Regional Science—New Concepts and Old Problems* Ed. E L Cripps (Pion, London) pp 109–125

Mathur P N, 1976 "New international economic order and resource allocation for developing countries" in *Environment, Regional Science, and Interregional Modelling* Eds M Chatterji, P von Rompuy (Springer, Berlin) pp 198–211

UNCTAD, 1976 "The dimensions of the required re-structuring of world manufacturing output and trade in order to reach the Lima target" TD/185/supplement 1, 12 April, United Nations Committee on Trade and Development, United Nations, New York

Labour Market Turnover: An Industrial Analysis of the Effects of Vacancies, Unemployment, and Firm Size

D GLEAVE, D PALMER
Centre for Environmental Studies, London

1 Introduction

In a complex, postindustrial society, which is characterised by increasing economic specialisation and an accelerating rate of structural change, the efficient matching of individual workers to individual jobs becomes harder to achieve. In recent years the relationship between the numbers of unemployed persons and vacant jobs has changed, such that for any given level of unemployment there are more vacant jobs than was previously the case. We consider it necessary to develop a fuller understanding of the nature of the matchmaking process and to advocate the application of policies which ameliorate mismatch if scarce resources are not to be squandered. The consequences of a low level of employment do not only concern workers and jobs but also mean that housing resources can be strained. This is because in areas where the demand for labour is exceptionally low, net out-migration of workers results in underutilisation of the housing stock. In other areas, where the prospects of employment are much better, chronic housing shortages often occur. Also, individual workers and their families suffer economic deprivation and psychological traumas whereas firms may be unable to achieve production targets because of a shortage of key workers. All of these problems occur in Britain today and although the causes cannot be solely attributed to mismatch, it is almost certainly true that mismatch exacerbates them. What is quite clear is that a high incidence of these problems in a localised area generates significant political repercussions, as is the case in the 'inner cities'.

Our aim in this paper is to examine the dynamic characteristics of the labour market, with particular emphasis on voluntary and involuntary turnover of workers and the effects of firm size on employment turnover. The movement of workers out of one job into another is associated with many other events, such as labour migration and occupational mobility. These events can be described and explained in terms of the changing distribution of employment opportunities in the space economy and structural changes in the demand for labour. However, as far as labour turnover is concerned, migration and occupational mobility are both fairly rare (but nonetheless extremely important) events. The majority of workers, when they change jobs or reenter employment after a period of economic activity or unemployment, retain their existing place of residence and their previous occupation. In this paper we focus attention on all workers who change jobs and probe the variations in turnover through time and by industry. We also examine the effects of variables which it has been suggested are major causal factors affecting the turnover process.

The dynamics of the labour market have been analysed by many authors in attempts to provide a theoretical understanding of how and why the problems mentioned above occur. Nonetheless, a coherent theory of the workings of the labour market, built on realistic assumptions of worker and management behaviour, has not yet been developed. There are a number of reasons for this. First, in our opinion there has been too little emphasis placed on feedback and recursive relationships, which are important characteristics of labour market processes. Instead there has been a strong reliance on simple linear descriptions. Second, each academic discipline with an interest in labour market systems has produced analytic frameworks which are clearly sectarian in interest. For example, geographers have tended to focus attention upon spatial aspects of labour market processes, by examining labour migration, and have not considered other aspects of turnover in great depth (see Johnson et al, 1974; Gleave and Cordey-Hayes, 1974; Goddard and Spence, 1976). Operations researchers have, inter alia, been concerned with the effect of labour turnover on individual firms, focussing attention on duration of stay (see Bartholomew, 1967; White, 1970; Blumen et al, 1955).

The decision to change job, whether taken voluntarily or involuntarily, and the consequent search for new employment, either in the same occupation/labour market or in a different occupation/labour market, is a complex behavioural process. Similarly, the decision to hire, promote, or fire labour is complex, but in almost all cases the effects are of interest to economists, sociologists, psychologists, geographers, operations researchers, and others. This suggests that a comprehensive understanding of the workings of the labour market requires an approach which is both dynamic and catholic, utilising concepts developed in a number of social science and applied science disciplines, if it is to be useful. However, this important point having been made, the difficulty of the task must not be underestimated. Many research problems are created, for example, by the lack of good data. There is a dearth of information on individual worker's job histories, and certain key variables, such as vacant jobs, are not measured with accuracy. In creating a realistic structure of labour market processes, it is often necessary to use linear methods of description which were criticised above in an attempt to identify key structural linkages. For these reasons and others it is not always possible within a single analytical framework to integrate research on such topics as internal labour markets, movement between firms, occupational mobility, labour migration, and the changing structure of labour demand. Nonetheless, this must be seen as an important goal.

In this paper, although we present some ideas which link up previous disparate studies and integrate different aspects of the labour market, we are chiefly concerned with the turnover of labour. More specifically, we examine the decisions of workers changing jobs and the effects of vacancies and firm size on the amount of turnover which is recorded. In the next section we comment on a number of theories of turnover which we try to explain in terms of a small number of key variables and concepts. We suggest that voluntary turnover is basically a process of risk minimisation. Most workers prefer to make career progressions (or even stay in employment) by remaining in the same area of residence and with the same employer, ceteris paribus. In the final section we present some findings which give support to our explanations and suggest how they can be improved.

2 Theoretical considerations

An evaluation of existing labour market theory could start at a number of different levels: the individual worker, the firm, the industry, or the national economy. Although this paper is mainly concerned with labour turnover at the industry level, and the effect of turnover rates of firm size and other variables, we consider it useful to identify the different ways in which individual workers quit jobs and are hired. This makes it easier to identify variables which explain different types of turnover.

2.1 Matchmaking and the individual search process

Figure 1 illustrates rather crudely a behaviour–decision-taking tree which applies to individual workers in a given plant. This diagram, which is concerned with *quit* rates, shows that two major types of quit may be identified: the voluntary quit and the involuntary quit. This distinction is of great theoretical importance because it draws particular attention to the possibility that employees in employment are, for a number of reasons, likely and able to fill vacancies elsewhere in the system without becoming unemployed. What is more, it shows that an individual's probability of quitting is partly contingent upon his/her ability to get another job. This, in turn, will probably be related to the number of suitable vacant jobs on offer and the number of other workers seeking them. It is not usually the case that workers leave the firm *before* seeking alternative employment. This point is mentioned because one of the classic models of the labour market, the Holt and David model (Holt and David, 1966), which considers aggregate interactions in the labour market, suggests that tenure formation occurs through the random interaction between unemployed workers and vacant jobs. The quit rate in their model is a linkage flow between the stock of employed workers and the stock of unemployed workers. Boorman's model of turnover (see White, 1970) goes further to suggest that not only are hirings a function of the number of unemployed and vacancies, as Holt and David suggest, but that quits are constant through time. Figure 1 suggests, more realistically, that quit rates are partially related to hire rates—at least in the case of workers moving straight from one job to another. However, Holt and David do acknowledge that a person can move 'almost immediately into a job vacancy' after quitting his previous job. This suggests that an instantaneous state of unemployment could be considered to characterise all workers moving between jobs. Nonetheless, this specification of workers' behaviour is still at substantive variance with reality. Their model articulates around the interaction process between unemployed persons and vacant jobs, and even if a short, or instantaneous, period of unemployment is allowed for, it does not contradict the fact that the matching of workers to jobs is a process which is occurring whilst many of the persons about to be hired *are still in employment*.

This particular criticism has been laboured somewhat for two important reasons. First, there is a strong relationship between quits and hirings, and until this is explicitly recognised no progress is possible towards understanding the dynamics of the labour market. Second, the two

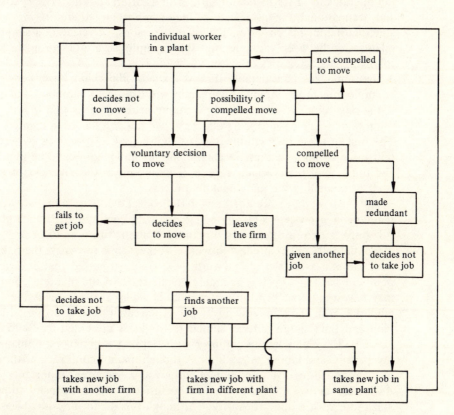

Figure 1. A job-turnover decision-taking tree which applies to individual workers.

models which have been reported, in suggesting random quit rates and
hirings from the stock of unemployed, fail to consider a very important
aspect of labour market dynamics. The matching of workers to jobs often
occurs within the firm and although this often means that vacancies may
not be notified outside the firm, the internal labour market can, when
working efficiently, contribute towards reducing mismatch.

The use of the unemployment variables in the Holt and David, and
Boorman models could be justified by the following argument. If a
vacant job is filled by a worker who was previously tenured then this will
create a new vacancy. The vacancy-chaining process will continue until a
vacant job is filled by an unemployed worker and consequently the
matchmaking process really does concern the relationship between vacant
jobs and unemployed workers. Such a suggestion is basically true much of
the time, but it must be remembered that during the process of vacancy
chaining, any of the vacancies created by labour turnover can be
withdrawn by an employer. Also, the chaining process can create a
vacancy either in a different labour market (if a successful candidate for a
job migrates in order to take it up), or in a different skill. The spatial
and occupational dimensions are of major importance therefore in
ameliorating mismatch. Nonetheless, our reasons for rejecting a simple
relationship between vacancies and the unemployed are based on the
following characteristics of vacancy chaining:
1 it often takes considerable time to exhaust the chain by either
   employing an unemployed worker or withdrawing a vacancy; and
2 the musical chairs effect of the chaining process means that *many
   vacancies* may be notified when only *one jew job* has been created.
The first of these reservations suggests that lagged relationships between
quit rates, hirings, tenures, vacancies, and unemployed should be used,
and the second that vacancy flow is as important as the vacancy stock
itself in modelling the matchmaking process.

Although we have been critical of Holt and David's notion that the
matchmaking process is mainly concerned with employing the unemployed,
it is only fair to say that they do consider labour turnover to be an
individual investment process in which workers seek to match their skills
with the best available jobs. [White (1970) has suggested that at different
points in the trade cycle, depending on the state of the market, labour
may have the upper hand in matchmaking, whilst at other times the
employer is in the strongest position.] The search process proposed by
Holt and David is, in outline, similar to the ideas presented by Renshaw
(1972). He relates labour turnover with learning experiences, human
investment, and labour migration. Although mainly concerned with job
changes which involve migration, Renshaw also makes an important
distinction between workers with an intrinsically high propensity to move
and those with a low propensity. Although this dichotomy had been
proposed earlier (see Blumen et al, 1955), it is the first time that those

with high employment mobility have been related to those with high geographic mobility, and forms the basis of Renshaw's theory that labour migration should be seen in terms of an extended local labour market. The high propensity of certain workers to migrate, it is argued, is contingent in the first instance upon their breaking the social and psychic ties of their formative environments. Another important factor is that these workers are also likely to be in possession of skills for which there is a low spatial employment opportunity density. Basically, this means that they are likely to be highly specialised, and in order to make a career progression may need to apply for jobs in distant labour markets. As well as possessing specialised skills, this class of highly mobile individuals would appear to be committed to improving their status, unlikely to suffer significant periods of unemployment, and more generally to be members of the primary labour market (see Doeringer and Poire, 1971; Poire, 1975; Gleave and Palmer, 1977), and hence male. In moving from one secure job to another they are also likely to set up a sequence of vacancy chains, which explains Renshaw's observation of 'cross-haul' migration. This theory, which is concerned with relating job turnover and migration, was developed by Gleave and Cordey-Hayes (1977), who suggested that high rates of turnover and migration depend on:

(1) the availability throughout the nation of a large number of vacant jobs, and

(2) a good knowledge, on the part of potential movers, of the vacancies concerned.

Quite clearly it is a theory which deals, by and large, with voluntary movers and requires integration with that part of labour market processes which explains how the unemployed are employed. First, though, we will consider in more detail the options available to the voluntary mover.

2.2 Mobility and firm size

The postwar period has seen, in virtually all industries, a tendency towards increased plant size, and more important a tendency towards monopoly ownership. This can be seen from the fact that

> "thirty years ago, the top hundred companies in Britain controlled only a fifth of manufacturing output and employment; now the share is around half" (Holland, 1978).

The potential voluntary mover with specialised skills is constrained by the number of job vacancies on the market at any one time, and by the velocity of turnover due to the vacancy-chaining process. However, it is probably the case that many vacancies do not enter the open labour market until they have circulated within the internal labour markets of firms (both within the same plant and between plants in the same firm). What is more, rapid growth of large firms, including the multinationals, probably means that an increasing proportion of vacant jobs are filled within the internal labour market, often as straight promotions. In most cases, workers who wish to improve their status, prospects, or salary are likely to do so in a way which minimises disturbance. Therefore a promotion within the same plant, because it will not necessitate rehousing, is a more attractive option than seeking better employment on the open job market. Even when a move to a different plant occurs, this may be preferable to changing firms. This need not be out of blind loyalty to the employer, but because the large firm is able, by virtue of its size, to provide a well-defined career profile for the individual worker. It will often be easier to achieve career progression within the large firm than by competing in the open labour market and moving between firms. The likelihood of within-firm and within-plant moves is likely to be a function of firm size because the matchmaking process is about relating workers with particular skills to jobs with a well-defined content. The larger the firm or plant, the greater the number of vacancies which will be suitable for any individual worker. The internal-promotions option is also reinforced by the behaviour of unions and management; by the former who increasingly insist that all vacancies should be filled by 'internal trawling', and by the latter who prefer internal appointments because of the capital they have invested in training and developing some of their employees.

2.3 The trade cycle: quits and hirings
We have argued above that a clear relationship exists between voluntary turnover, vacancy chains, and the internal labour markets of firms. We now address ourselves to the problem of how labour turnover varies through the trade cycle, paying particular attention to the ratios of voluntary and involuntary quits and hirings. (For the purposes of this paper we define a voluntary hiring to be a person who has secured a new job before quitting the previous job whilst an involuntary hiring is a person who takes up a job from the ranks of the unemployed or economically inactive.) We assume that most of the time the system dynamics are largely determined by vacancies, and furthermore that the demand for labour is associated with product demand within the general economy. This means that voluntary turnover will take on a cyclical trend through time with most moves occurring when most vacancies occur. Many of these moves, particularly in industries dominated by large firms, will occur within the internal labour market and are not recorded. Multiplant firms will therefore generate most interplant moves (labour migration) towards the peak of the trade cycle when demand for labour is greatest. However, in addition there will be a steady stream of interplant movements, which is more regular, due to the aging of the firm's labour force and regular internal promotions.

The hiring of unemployed labour, largely skilled, semi-skilled, and unskilled workers, plus certain white-collar and service grades, will also vary through the trade cycle. When vacancies are low, voluntary mobility of employed workers will be low, but so will hirings of the unemployed. At the peak of the trade cycle, firms will not collectively be able to satisfy their total demand for labour from the existing stock of employed workers and will therefore make many hirings from the ranks of the unemployed and economically inactive. The hiring of unemployed workers, therefore, will peak at the same time as voluntary turnover peaks and trough at the same time. However, the proportions of hirings coming from the ranks of the employed and unemployed may not stay constant. When few vacancies obtain, firms will have the upper hand in the matchmaking process, being able to select from large numbers of job applicants. In all probability this means that the majority of hirings will come from the ranks of the employed. The hiring cycle we hypothesise, but do not test, is illustrated in figure 2.

It is more difficult to suggest how labour quits will vary through time but we start off in this task by considering the total relationship between quits and hirings. Boorman's model of labour turnover allows for variable levels of recruitment but constant rates of quits. This hypothesis is particularly interesting becasue it is analogous to the Lansing and Mueller (1967) model of geographic mobility. They argued that regional out-migration rates were constant but that in-migration rates were variable, favouring the regions of fast growth. The hypothesis of constant quit rates is tested in the next section along with an alternative hypothesis which is also analogous to a theory from migration research.

Cordey-Hayes and Gleave (1974) found that the cross-sectional relationship between the components of migration was positive in Great Britain. The process which explained this characteristic was mobility in an extended (not local) labour market. Before in-movement occurs, out-movement must preceed it in most cases. In turn, out-migration requires a vacant or newly created job and a vacant or newly built house to occur elsewhere. We suggest that a similar, serial relationship can occur between

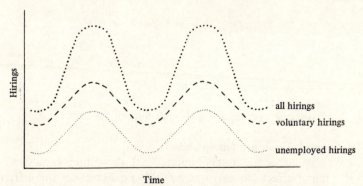

Figure 2. Variations in hiring rates through the trade cycle.

quits and hirings and that the relationship is positive because of the
importance of voluntary turnover. However, this hypothesis requires
total quits to reach a maximum at the employment peak of the trade
cycle and appears counterintuitive. We can only resolve this dilemma by
considering the relationship between voluntary quits and involuntary quits,
bearing in mind that voluntary quits are also voluntary hirings and that
redundancies and layoffs reach a peak in the trough of the trade cycle.
Three reasonable possibilities exist which are illustrated in figure 3, the
first of which resolves our dilemma. They are:
(a) voluntary and involuntary quits are negatively associated but the
     former dominate;
(b) voluntary and involuntary quits are negatively associated but neither
     dominate (the Boorman hypothesis);
(c) voluntary and involuntary quits are negatively associated but the
     latter dominate.
We favour hypothesis (a) because annual turnover rates of labour show a
positive correlation with growth rates, thereby indicating a positive
relationship between hirings and quits. Since we have asserted a particular
cyclical pattern of hirings, quit rates should exhibit a similar but dampened
trend.

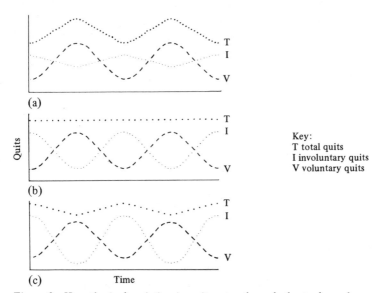

Key:
T total quits
I involuntary quits
V voluntary quits

Figure 3. Hypothesised variation in quits rates through the trade cycle.

2.4 The turnover of male and female labour
So far we have argued at a very general level about how vacancies and
firm size might affect labour turnover. We now consider the different
behaviour of male and female workers.

The effects and ramifications of voluntary turnover are mainly associated with the primary labour market (see Gleave and Palmer, 1977). They imply a well-defined notion of career progression and suggest rational behaviour within a minimum-risk framework. In fact, most job opportunities within this domain are taken up by male workers. Consequently, we expect the hypothesised effects of firm size and opportunities within the internal labour markets of firms to determine the behaviour of male employees. Female employees, with their higher rates of entering and leaving the labour market, are likely to be affected by other considerations. The majority of female workers are to be found within the age range of thirty-five to sixty years, and most of them are married. They are likely therefore to be constrained to some extent by the employment decisions of their husbands and the fact that many families still consider female income to be marginal, though often necessary. Similarly, employers often adopt policies which result in married female labour being laid off before males when the labour force is contracted. This means that far fewer women adopt career aspirations, so the firm-size variable is likely to be less significant in explaining female turnover of labour. Female workers are more susceptible to the crude interplay of market forces, taking up employment when vacancies are numerous and being induced to take work at low wages when unemployed. Ironically, we think the simplistic matchmaking model of Holt and David is far more applicable to the behaviour of women in the labour market than that of men.

From the discussion so far we conclude that:

1 First and foremost, labour turnover is strongly determined by the availability of vacancies, which gives labour the opportunity to maximise job satisfaction and income at minimum risk.

2 The majority of quits and hirings are voluntary, affecting workers (mainly males) who are already in employment.

3 This, in turn, suggests a strong positive relationship between hirings and quits.

4 Many individual workers who turn over voluntarily have fairly well-defined career aspirations which can often be satisfied within the firm (so long as it is large). Therefore the amount of recorded (voluntary) turnover will be negatively associated with firm size.

5 Female workers are more likely to be subjected to the vagaries of the labour market. Because of the dominant societal role of males and a tendency for females to attend to family responsibilities, female workers are usually considered by employers, their husbands, and themselves as secondary wage earners. Consequently, they will take up employment when many vacancies occur or be induced onto the labour market when those in desparate need for extra family income record high levels of female unemployment.

3 Empirical results

This section is divided into two main parts and reports variations in hiring and quit rates between industries (the cross-sectional analysis) and the same variations through time. Before outlining our findings, we discuss the data which were used in our analyses.

Two sets of data were collected which measured turnover on the one hand and vacancy, unemployment, and firm size on the other. The first set served as dependent variables and the second set as independent variables. The turnover data, vacancy data, and unemployment data were disaggregated by industry and sex, whilst the 'firm-size' data were disaggregated by industry only. Labour turnover was measured in four ways from two separate sources:

(1) Annual hiring rates. These were expressed as the percentage of workers employed by their current employer for less than twelve months from one April to the next and obtained for 1972 and 1973 from the Department of Employment's New Earnings Survey.

(2) Monthly hiring rates, monthly quit rates, and monthly turnover, the sum of the two, were obtained quarterly from October 1970 to April 1974 except for January 1972. These data were obtained from the *Department of Employment Gazette* (HMSO, London) but only the April data for 1972 and 1973 were used in the cross-sectional regression analysis reported below.

With regard to the independent variables, two data sources were used to collect these:

(1) Information on numbers employed, vacant jobs, and employees in employment were collected for April 1972 and April 1973 from the *Department of Employment Gazette* and adjusted to percentages of employees in employment.

(2) Information on 'firm size' were collected from the Department of Industry's *Business Monitor* (PA 1003; HMSO, London) for the years 1972 and 1973. Two statistics were used—the percentage of firms with less than a hundred workers and the percentage of workers employed by firms with less than a hundred workers.

3.1 Cross-sectional analysis: turnover, firm size, and vacancies

Twenty-four simple regression analyses were attempted in order to identify the cross-sectional industrial relationship between each of the turnover statistics and the four independent variables. They were conducted for male, female, and total workers for the years 1972 and 1973 and the results are reported in table 1. The purpose of this exercise was to identify important cross-sectional linkages, given the quality of existing data and the method of collecting them. It was not anticipated that a robust equation system that could be used for predicted purposes would result. We were unable to say whether variations in vacancies between industries would generate cross-sectional regression relationships which would be similar to the serial relationships postulated in the previous section. On the one hand the variation in vacancies between industries might well produce the same effects as variations through time. However, it could also be argued that, despite the long-run differences in the employment trajectories of industries, in the short run, employment prospects in all industries are more strongly affected by the state of the trade cycle. In this case, although there would still be

Table 1. Cross-sectional relationships between turnover and vacancy rates, unemployment rates, employment size, and firm size.

Male 1972

Annhire	=	$7 \cdot 19 + 25 \cdot 17$ wkrsize;	$R^2 = 0 \cdot 783$
Mnthire	=	$1 \cdot 13 + 3 \cdot 22$ wkrsize;	$R^2 = 0 \cdot 459$
Mntquit	=	$0 \cdot 03 + 1 \cdot 70$ vacancy $+ 0 \cdot 22$ unmplmnt;	$R^2 = 0 \cdot 808$
Mntturn	=	$2 \cdot 46 + 6 \cdot 08$ wkrsize;	$R^2 = 0 \cdot 591$

Male 1973

Annhire	=	$9 \cdot 87 + 30 \cdot 59$ wkrsize;	$R^2 = 0 \cdot 664$
Mnthire[a]	=	$1 \cdot 58 + 2 \cdot 14$ wkrsize;	$R^2 = 0 \cdot 263$
Mntquit	=	$1 \cdot 66 + 2 \cdot 16$ wkrsize;	$R^2 = 0 \cdot 397$
Mntturn[a]	=	$3 \cdot 24 + 4 \cdot 76$ wkrsize;	$R^2 = 0 \cdot 346$

Female 1972

Annhire	=	$-6 \cdot 41 + 33 \cdot 12$ firmsize;	$R^2 = 0 \cdot 265$
Mnthire	=	$-0 \cdot 67 + 1 \cdot 97$ unmplmnt;	$R^2 = 0 \cdot 381$
Mntquit		no computation	
Mntturn	=	$0 \cdot 98 + 2 \cdot 73$ unmplmnt;	$R^2 = 0 \cdot 282$

Female 1973

Annhire	=	$13 \cdot 45 + 5 \cdot 27$ vacancy;	$R^2 = 0 \cdot 390$
Mnthire		no computation	
Mntquit		no computation	
Mntturn		no computation	

Total 1972

Annhire	=	$9 \cdot 41 + 6 \cdot 78$ vacancy;	$R^2 = 0 \cdot 663$
Mnthire	=	$1 \cdot 45 + 1 \cdot 00$ vacancy;	$R^2 = 0 \cdot 470$
Mntquit	=	$1 \cdot 62 + 0 \cdot 88$ vacancy;	$R^2 = 0 \cdot 527$
Mntturn	=	$3 \cdot 07 + 1 \cdot 89$ vacancy;	$R^2 = 0 \cdot 527$

Total 1973

Annhire	=	$9 \cdot 37 + 5 \cdot 77$ vacancy;	$R^2 = 0 \cdot 666$
Mnthire	=	$1 \cdot 64 + 0 \cdot 51$ vacancy;	$R^2 = 0 \cdot 344$
Mntquit	=	$1 \cdot 65 + 0 \cdot 49$ vacancy;	$R^2 = 0 \cdot 484$
Mntturn	=	$3 \cdot 28 + 1 \cdot 00$ vacancy;	$R^2 = 0 \cdot 426$

[a] Insignificant at $F = 9 \cdot 33$, significant at $F = 4 \cdot 75$.

Annhire is annual hiring rate; mnthire is monthly hiring rate; mntquit is monthly quit rate; mntturn is the sum of the previous two; vacancy is vacancy rate; unmplmnt is unemployment rate; wkrsize is the proportion of an industry's labour force employed in firms with <100 employees; firmsize is the proportion of firms with <100 employees.

variations between industries in vacancy rates, the inability of workers to move between industries (because of occupational mobility constraints) might result in a poor relationship between turnover and vacancies. The exceptions could be at the employment margin, in female employment. What we did expect, particularly in the case of male employment, was a strong relationship between turnover and industrial variations in firm size.

The regression results for male workers provide support for our contention that the firm size is an important determinant of labour turnover. Of the eight regressions performed for 1972 and 1973, six were significant at an F value of $9\cdot33$ and of these, firm size, in the guise of the 'wkrsize' variable, described the greatest variance in all but one case. The monthly quit rate in 1972 was instead associated with the industrial rate of vacancies and unemployment. Even in this case there was a strong zero-order correlation between monthly quits and 'wkrsize', which in this case alone was smaller than that between quits and vacancies ($0\cdot736$ against $0\cdot782$). The coefficient of determination was greater than $0\cdot59$ in all significant cases except one, which, considering that only the independent variable entered these regressions (apart from the exception already mentioned), suggests that the firm-size structure of industries has an important effect on short-run labour market behaviour. It is also worth mentioning that in the case of the 1972 results, the wkrsize regression coefficient for annual hirings is less than twelve times that for monthly hirings. This could be due to anomalous behaviour in the particular month under scrutiny. However, it is more likely to be due to the effects of the distribution of times of completed service with firms. This simply means that a proportion of workers both will be hired and will quit during the same financial year and are not therefore enumerated as an annual hiring.

In some respects, the results for females are more interesting than those for males. In only one case did either of the variables representing the effects of firm size within the industry enter any of the regressions which were computed. In fact, only one regression was computed which satisfied our criterion of an F value of $9\cdot33$ or greater ($p = 0\cdot01$). The other results which are reported in table 1 are regressions in which the entry criterion was modified to an F value of $4\cdot75$ ($p = 0\cdot05$) simply to see which variables might affect labour turnover at a very low level of significance. Basically, we conclude that variable turnover behaviour in the female labour market is not strongly associated by any of the variables assumed to be of theoretical importance—at least not in terms of our industrial cross-sectional results. Without the benefit of further analysis we can only speculate why this may have been so. One possibility is that the vacancy variable was insignificant because of structural unemployment amongst females. This would mean that unemployed and inactive women were unable to take up vacant jobs because they were not skilled in the occupations for which there was a labour demand. A second possibility is that the unemployment variable was insignificant because of differential rates of registration. It is well known that unemployed single women tend to register as unemployed whereas married women do not (and therefore become economically inactive). If the proportions of married and unmarried women vary strongly between industries this could explain a poor relationship between turnover—especially quits—and unemployment. In the case of firm-size effects we have already postulated that these ought not to be significant in the female labour market and this contention is therefore supported by the 'non-results' of the regression analysis.

When the male and female labour markets were combined, seven significant regressions were obtained, each of which indicated that vacancies was the single important variable affecting turnover rates. This was not altogether surprising. We had previously argued that vacancy rates are the principal generator of labour market turnover, particularly through time. However, we did not speculate on the effect of vacancies in the cross-sectional analysis although it seemed reasonable to suppose that turnover and chaining would be high in those faster-growth industries with most vacancies. What requires more explanation is why vacancies was the important variable in total labour market regressions but not in the male and female subsectors. Our view is that the two subsectors are homogeneous and function quite differently because of the different needs and aspirations of male and female workers. However, from the perspective of employers the two subsectors are quite complementary in that they provide workers for different types of job.

The zero-order correlations in the male case show that vacancies were of secondary importance to employment size. The same correlations in the female case show that vacancies were of secondary importance to unemployment (in most cases). When the cross-sectional data were combined the result was that the independent variable which was second most important in both the male and female cases exhibited the greatest correlations with turnover. This fact also implies that the firm size was poorly related to turnover in the female labour market and that unemployment was poorly related to turnover in the male labour market.

One final comment must be made about interpreting the results of the regression analyses reported above. We have already said that we do not consider them to be sufficiently robust to be used for forecasting future turnover. Therefore, they quite clearly cannot be used to provide firm verification of the hypotheses we have formulated. It could be the case that other variables are more important in explaining labour turnover; variables which we have overlooked in our analysis. The effect of the inclusion of other variables could be to discredit the arguments we have made. However, in our view this is unlikely to be the case. The most important independent variable that was omitted was wages but this particular variable generates many problems when included in regression analyses. It is often wrongly signed, suggesting that workers are quitting high-wage industries and regions. In fact what happens is that the mobile workers concerned move into jobs which are better paid than their previous jobs, in industries which pay less on average. That is to say, the variables used to represent wage are industry-wide averages whereas the mobile workers apply for particular jobs at particular rates of pay.

3.2 Time series analysis: quits and hirings
The time series analysis was concerned exclusively with the relationship between hiring rates and quit rates and does not take account of variations in firm size through time. In fact the overall process of increasing firm size which appears to be occurring in all industries did not produce significant changes over the period of analysis, October 1970 to April 1974. In any case, our hypotheses about the effects of firm size on turnover were about variations between industries rather than through time. What we did postulate in the previous section was a positive serial relationship between quits and hirings. We argued that since voluntary quits are, by and large, reflected by immediate hirings, the principal exceptions being retirements and women having children, what was being tested by this hypothesis was the time series relationship between voluntary quits and redundancies. This is because 'voluntary turnover hiring' and hirings from the stock of the unemployed are positively associated; although we cannot prove the relationship shown in figure 2, it is almost inconceivable that a nonpositive relationship between these variables could occur. The only debate concerns the relative importance of the two variables at different points in the trade cycle. We showed in figure 3 that three possible relationships could obtain between voluntary quits (firings and redundancies). We argued that in all cases a negative relationship between the two terms would obtain, otherwise this would mean that firings and redundancies peaked when hirings peaked which is clearly very improbable (not to say ridiculous). The question therefore becomes one about which of the two terms dominates total quits. Our hypothesis of a positive relationship between total quits and hirings requires that voluntary quits dominate whilst the Boorman hypothesis suggests that neither dominates. If involuntary quits were most important, then a negative relationship would obtain between quits and hirings. The easiest of these hypotheses to test from turnover data is the second, simply because it means that quit rates are invariant through time. Figure 4 shows the quit rates for both male and female employment for all employees in manufacturing industry and for four selected industries. This shows quite unequivocally that quit rates are not invariant through time. Although one particular observation, that for July 1972, was characterised by unexpectedly low quit rates the rest of the series still displays serial fluctuation. Of course, this could be attributable to the

bizarre employment trends of the 'Barber boom'[1], but the trend before this phenomenon of late 1972 and 1973 and before July 1972 displays fairly consistent falls in quit rates. This suggests that on the limited evidence available the Boorman hypothesis should be rejected and hypotheses (a) and (c) of figure 3 evaluated.

Our test of these hypotheses centres around the relationship between quits and hirings because of our inability to separate voluntary and involuntary quits. Figure 5 shows the relationship between quits and hirings for all manufacturing industry over the period October 1970 to April 1974. The observation for July 1972 is strongly affected by the low quit rate of that month which, if excluded, results in a strong positive relationship between quits and hirings over the whole period. The regression line suggests that both hirings and firings are highest when the former are dominant and so supports our hypothesis that voluntary and involuntary firings are negatively associated over the trade cycle, with the former dominating the total trend. There is no suggestion whatsoever of a negative relationship. This confirms our notion that when the trade cycle is on the downturn and bottoming out, from about October 1970 to April 1972 in the case of our observations, then quits exceed hirings. The results are not so unequivocal about the upturn when we would expect hirings to dominate quits. Excluding the observation for July

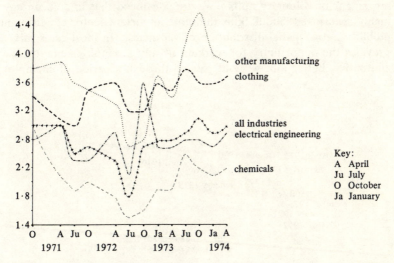

Figure 4. Serial variations in monthly quits rates: all manufacturing industries and selected industries for all employees.

[1] The 'Barber boom' describes the effects of the economic policies used by the Conservative administration of 1970–1974 during the latter half of its period in office. Chancellor Anthony Barber implemented a policy of rapid expansion of the money supply, which created many vacancies but also caused rapid inflation, first in the land and property sector and then throughout the British economy.

1972 we can see from figure 5 that in only four of the remaining twelve observations hirings are greater than quits. It is almost certain that this apparently poor result would have been worse had data for January 1971 and January 1972 been available. However, the four observations in question, for January 1973, October 1973, and April 1974, all occurred during the upturn or levelling out of the turnover cycle. It is possible that this positive linear turnover relationship was (in terms of the location of observations) reflecting or anticipating the trend towards increased levels of unemployment. This could explain the dominance of net quits over the total period.

Finally, it is worthwhile noting the similarity between the serial relationship shown in figure 5 and a similar cross-sectional association in the case of interregional labour migration. Both sets of observations suggest a dynamic behaviour system, largely dominated by random turnover where gross movement is high in relation to net shifts. They also suggest that net 'in-movement' occurs during periods of expansion and in regions of greatest overall growth. We now feel secure in suggesting that gross turnover only appears random at the aggregate level. At the scale of the individual household, 'cross-haul' moves provide the opportunity for both sets of mover to benefit. This will occur because better job opportunities are either created, or become vacant through retirement or voluntary quits. We are convinced that in an economy with highly specialized labour skills the most important factor conditioning mobility is the spatial distribution of vacancies. In most cases this provides the opportunity for workers already in employment to seek alternative, better jobs without passing through a period of unemployment.

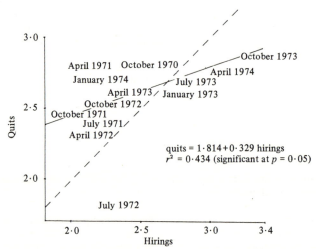

Figure 5. The serial relationship between quits and hirings for all manufacturing industries for all employees.

The extent to which these moves result in movement between firms depends upon the size of the firms within industries, the extent of employers' monopoly and the spatial distribution of employment opportunities for a given class of workers.

References
Bartholomew D J, 1967 *Stochastic Models for Social Processes* (John Wiley, Chichester, Sussex)
Blumen I, Kogan M, McCarthy P J, 1955 *The Industrial Mobility of Labour as a Probability Process* (Cornell University Press, Ithaca, NY)
Cordey-Hayes M, Gleave D, 1974 "Migration movements and the differential growth of city regions in England and Wales" *Papers of the Regional Science Association* 3 99–126
Doeringer P B, Poire M J, 1971 *Internal Labour Markets and Manpower Analysis* (D C Heath, Lexington, Mass)
Gleave D, 1977 "Unemployment types, vacancy data and the demand for labour" WN-457, Centre for Environmental Studies, London
Gleave D, Cordey-Hayes M, 1974 "Inter urban migration seen as an extension of the local labour market" WN-399, Centre for Environmental Studies, London
Gleave D, Cordey-Hayes M, 1977 *Progress in Planning, Volume 8 Migration Dynamics and Labour Market Turnover* (Pergamon Press, Oxford) pp 1–95
Gleave D, Palmer D, 1977 "Labour mobility and the dynamics of labour market turnover" paper presented to the 17th Congress, European Regional Science Association, Krakow, Poland; WN-460, Centre for Environmental Studies, London
Goddard J B, Spence N A, 1976 "The national system of cities as a framework for regional development research in Britain: some preliminary thoughts and empirical results on employment trends in British labour market areas" paper presented to British Regional Science Association, University College London
Holland S, 1978 quoted in *Sunday Times Business Supplement* 27 August
Holt C C, David M H, 1966 "The concept of job vacancies in a dynamic theory of the labour market" in *The Measurement and Interpretation of Job Vacancies* (National Bureau of Economic Research; Columbia University Press, New York) pp 73–110
Johnson J H, Salt J, Wood P, 1974 *Housing and the Migration of Labour in England and Wales* (Saxon House, Teakfield, Farnborough, Hants)
Lansing J B, Mueller E, 1967 "The geographical mobility of labour" Surrey Research Centre, Institute for Social Research, Ann Arbor, Mich.
Poire M J, 1975 "Notes for a theory of labour market stratification" in *Labour Market Stratification* Eds R L Edwards, M Reich, D M Gordon (Lexington Books, D C Heath, Lexington, Mass)
Renshaw V, 1972 "Labour mobility, turnover and gross migration" faculty WP-1, Bureau of Business Research, University of Nebraska, Lincoln
Thirlwall A P, 1974 "Types of unemployment in the regions of Great Britain" paper 4, Department of Economics, School of Economic and Social Studies, University of Manchester, England
White H C, 1970 *Chains of Opportunity: System Models of Mobility in Organisations* (Harvard University Press, Cambridge, Mass)

A Time-series Analysis of Population and Employment Change in the West Midlands

D BOOTH, G HYMAN
Centre for Environmental Studies

1 Introduction

Regional scientists who analyse local economic change conventionally recognise two distinctions which are broadly complementary. The first distinction is made between industries according to their functional significance in a specific local economic system. Industries whose activity changes in a manner which is not affected by the rest of the local economy are categorised as *basic industries*, whereas the others are sometimes misleadingly called 'service' industries but can best be referred to as *nonbasic industries* (Lowry, 1964; Barras et al, 1971; Batty, 1976). The second distinction is made between local economic systems and relates to the degree to which local employment changes are a reflection of the local industrial mix or of factors unique to the local economy. The former component of employment change can be referred to as *proportional change*, the latter as *differential change* (Brown, 1972).

By making these distinctions regional scientists recognise that local changes in employment in specific industries are affected by changes in the activity of other local industries and that the structure of such relations of cause and effect can differ between local economic systems. Such considerations motivate both the identification of local systems of causal relations between industrial activities and the comparative study of identified local variants of these systems.

In this paper systems of this kind are identified by the estimation of predictive models by use of time-series data. For the types of models used in this paper the distinction between basic and nonbasic activities is central, whereas the distinction between proportional and differential change is peripheral.

Related to the question of the economic base is the role of population changes. "Population began to be seen as an integral part of the fabric of change. At a transitional point references to the constant 'interaction' between population and economy hinted that the causal chain might be complex" (Eversley, 1965, page 23). The causal structure of the Lowry model incorporates population changes as shown in figure 1. This causal

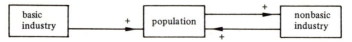

Figure 1. The causal structure of the Lowry model.

structure represents basic industry as exogenous, and population and nonbasic industry as mutually reinforcing endogenous processes.

The possibility of unemployment arising is not considered explicitly in the Lowry model. Implicit assumptions that the model user could make might be the continued expansion of basic industry, or the instantaneous adjustment of labour supply to an equilibrium in relation to basic-sector activity. Neither assumption seems to be realistic and the treatment of unemployment as a component of the model clearly requires empirical investigation (Sayer, 1976).

The models presented in this paper are restricted in terms of their application to policy appraisal. Policies should be regarded as causes of change in the processes being analysed, and both need to be represented by time-series data. Neither the treatment of policy as a residual effect nor as a form of time dependence arising in the parameters of a deterministic model is a satisfactory basis for appraisal. The reader interested in further exploring the links between time-series models and economic policy is strongly recommended to look at the report of the Select Committee on Policy Optimisation (Ball, 1978).

2 Model estimation

2.1 The model form

The general mathematical form of the model being used is given by the equation

$$X_j(t) = \sum_{n=1}^{N} \sum_{i=1}^{J} C_{ij}(n) X_i(t-n) + B_j + \epsilon_j(t) \,, \tag{1}$$

where

$X_j(t)$ refers to the value of component process j as it develops over time t;

$C_{ij}(n)$ represents the effect of component i on component j after a time lag of n periods;

B_j is a constant element of the component process $X_j(t)$;

$\epsilon_j(t)$ denotes the *innovations* in the process $X_j(t)$, and represents those variations which cannot be predicted from the past values of any of the components;

N is an integer denoting the maximum time lag of the effects being analysed and is referred to as the *model order*, and

J is the number of components.

The use of a model of this form for the analysis of causal relations is based on the theory of feedback between stationary stochastic processes: see, for example, Granger (1969), Sims (1972), Caines and Chan (1975a; 1975b), Caines and Sethi (1977), Pierce and Hough (1977), Hyman (1977), Hyman and Booth (1978a), Hyman and Palmer (1978). The main feature to note in the form of the model is the way it incorporates feedback properties. When coefficients in equation (1) of the type $C_{ij}(n)$

and $C_{ji}(m)$ are both nonzero there is said to be *feedback* between the process i and the process j. The $C_{ij}(n)$ form an $N \times J \times J$ array $\mathbf{C}$ made up of the N matrices $\mathbf{C}(n)$—see equation (5) in section 3—stacked one on top of the other. When the graph of the structure of $\mathbf{C}$ contains no cycles, the joint process is said to be *feedback free*. These definitions conform to the weak sense of feedback freedom used in Caines (1976). The process X_i *causes* the process X_j wherever $C_{ij}(n)$ is nonzero for some positive integer n.

2.2 The estimation method

The model parameters $C_{ij}(n)$ and B_j are estimated separately for each process j by use of time-series observations on each component. The method of estimation minimises the variance of the innovations, $\mathrm{var}(\epsilon_j)$. The innovations consequently have zero expectation,

$$E(\epsilon_j) = 0 . \tag{2}$$

They also satisfy the conditions

$$\mathrm{cov}[X_i(s), \epsilon_j(t)] = 0 , \ s < t , \quad \text{and} \quad \mathrm{cov}[\epsilon_i(s), \epsilon_j(t)] = 0 , \ s \neq t . \tag{3}$$

Contemporaneous innovations can be mutually correlated, and we define

$$\sigma_{ij} = \mathrm{cov}[\epsilon_i(t), \epsilon_j(t)] . \tag{4}$$

When $\sigma_{ij} \neq 0$ the processes X_i and X_j are said to be *coupled*.

The model parameters are estimated by use of a standard multiple-regression package (Nie et al, 1975) with the stepwise-entry option. Inclusion of variables is determined by an F test, which is usually set for a significance level of 1%. The innovations' covariance structure is estimated by calculating a Pearson correlation matrix between the residuals of the regressions.

2.3 The spatial system

In order to avoid the need to give detailed consideration to the inter-dependence between industrial and residential location, an extensively researched subject, it was decided to study whole geographical territories which were self-contained with respect to journeys between home and work. Three experiments in designing self-contained areas for the UK have been conducted: the *city regions* used by Fielding (1971), the *Standard Metropolitan Labour Areas* (SMLAs) used by Drewett et al (1974), and the *labour-market areas* used by Smart (1974). The third design provides the basis for the design of *travel-to-work areas* adopted by the Department of Employment (1970) and which are used in the present West Midlands research as study areas. Travel-to-work areas are smaller than either city regions or SMLAs, and self-containment applies both to residences and workplaces.

In the West Midlands the travel-to-work areas correspond fairly closely to the present metropolitan districts. This correspondence enables demographic and employment data sources to be integrated without difficulty for time periods subsequent to local-government reorganisation in 1974. Since the West Midlands districts experienced boundary changes in 1966, only a minor exercise in area aggregation is needed to obtain demographic data for comparable areas to the present districts. Prior to 1966 more substantial aggregations are needed. For both sets of boundary changes the constituent parts of the newly formed areas can be gleaned from Municipal Year Books. Details are given in table 2 of Hyman and Booth (1978b) for the five districts Birmingham, Dudley, Sandwell (West Bromwich), Walsall, and Wolverhampton.

2.4 The component processes

For each study area the state of the system at each midyear is characterised by annual changes in employment in sixteen industrial categories plus the annual change in adult unemployment, the level of annual net migration, and the level of annual natural population change. In addition the annual changes in male, female, and total employment are included, to make twenty-two components in all. Clearly two of the employment-change components are redundant, but have been included in the analysis to investigate alternative schemes for forecasting aggregate employment changes.

Table 1. The twenty-two components.

Notation	Description	1968 order
A	Primary	I, II
B1	Metal manufacturing	VI
B2	Mechanical engineering	VII, X
B3	Electrical engineering	VIII, IX
B4	Vehicles	XI
B5	Metal goods	XII
B6	Food, drink, and tobacco	III
B7	Chemicals	IV, V
B8	Rest of manufacturing	XIII to XIX
C	Construction	XX
D	Utilities	XXI
E	Distribution	XXIII
F	Miscellaneous services	XXVI
G	Public administration	XXVII
H	Transport	XXII
I	Insurance, professional, and scientific	XXIV, XXV
N	Natural population change	
M	Net migration	
U	Adult unemployment	
E_M	Male employment	
E_F	Female employment	
E_T	Total employment	

Annual migratory change is estimated from data on local-authority populations, births, and deaths published in the Registrar General's Statistical Review and, for recent years, in Local Authority Vital Statistics. Prior to model estimation these estimates need to be adjusted to eliminate the effect of small errors in population estimates that accumulate between census years. The procedure used is described in detail in the appendix to Hyman and Booth (1978b). A discussion of some of the ramifications of the presence of these accumulating errors is available in Hyman (1978).

The sixteen industrial categories are the groupings of industrial orders in the 1968 Standard Industrial Classification (Department of Employment, 1972) given in table 1. Their relation to the 1958 and 1948 Standard Industrial Classifications (Shenfield, 1967; Department of Employment, 1965) is described in Hyman and Booth (1978b).

3 Forecasting

The exposition of the results presented in this section is facilitated by the adoption of a compact notation. For each time lag n define the coefficient matrices $C(n)$ from the coefficients in equation (1) by

$$C(n) = \begin{bmatrix} C_{11}(n) & \cdots & C_{J1}(n) \\ \vdots & & \vdots \\ C_{1J}(n) & \cdots & C_{JJ}(n) \end{bmatrix}. \tag{5}$$

Then equation (1) can be written in the form

$$X(t) = \sum_{n=1}^{N} C(n)X(t-n) + B + \epsilon(t), \tag{6}$$

where $X(t)$ is the J-component instantaneous state vector with components $X_j(t)$, B is the vector of constants B_j, and $\epsilon(t)$ is the vector of innovations $\epsilon_j(t)$, $j = 1, ..., J$. An additional degree of compactness can be achieved by defining the *vintage representation*, with a coefficient matrix of the form

$$A = \begin{bmatrix} C(1) & C(2) & \cdots & C(N-1) & C(N) \\ I & 0 & \cdots & 0 & 0 \\ 0 & I & \cdots & 0 & 0 \\ \vdots & & & & \vdots \\ 0 & 0 & \cdots & I & 0 \end{bmatrix}, \tag{7}$$

where I is the $J \times J$ identity matrix and 0 is the $J \times J$ zero matrix, and state descriptions

$$\overline{X}(t) = \begin{bmatrix} X(t) \\ X(t-1) \\ \vdots \\ X(t+1-N) \end{bmatrix}, \quad \overline{B} = \begin{bmatrix} B \\ 0 \\ \vdots \\ 0 \end{bmatrix}, \quad \text{and} \quad \overline{\epsilon}(t) = \begin{bmatrix} \epsilon(t) \\ 0 \\ \vdots \\ 0 \end{bmatrix}, \tag{8}$$

where there are $N-1$ 0s in $\overline{B}$ and $\overline{\epsilon}(t)$. Equation (6) can now be expressed as

$$\overline{X}(t) = \mathbf{A}\overline{X}(t-1) + \overline{B} + \overline{\epsilon}(t) . \tag{9}$$

To elaborate the computation of forecasts it is convenient to assume that the history of the system is known up to and including time $t = 0$. We wish to compute forecasts and their uncertainties for positive times. The forecasts are defined as the conditional expectations

$$\hat{\overline{X}}(k) = \mathrm{E}[\overline{X}(k)|\overline{X}(0)] .$$

By use of the linearity of the expectation operator and equation (2), the following recursive formulae can be deduced:

$$\left.\begin{aligned} \hat{\overline{X}}(1) &= \mathbf{A}\overline{X}(0) + \overline{B} , \\ \hat{\overline{X}}(k+1) &= \mathbf{A}\hat{\overline{X}}(k) + \overline{B} ; \end{aligned}\right\} \tag{10}$$

these are used for computation.

The uncertainties in these forecasts are obtained as follows. Define the *deviation* process

$$D(k) = X(k) - \hat{X}(k) . \tag{11}$$

The uncertainties of these forecasts are based on the covariance structure of the deviation process. For k greater than N, let

$$\mathrm{var}[\overline{D}(k)] = \overline{\overline{\mathbf{W}}}(k, k)$$

$$= \begin{bmatrix} W(k, k) & W(k, k-1) & \cdots & W(k, k+1-N) \\ W(k-1, k) & & & \cdot \\ \vdots & & & \vdots \\ W(k+1-N, k) & \cdot & \cdots & W(k+1-N, k+1-N) \end{bmatrix}, \tag{12}$$

where

$$W(l, m) = \mathrm{cov}[D(l), D(m)] . \tag{13}$$

The diagonal elements $W(l, l)$ are of course the predicted error variances for forecasts l steps ahead. Note that, unlike the innovations process, the deviation process may covary with its own history. The deviation process does not, however, covary with the future of the innovations process. The deviation process's covariance structure has a natural vintage representation as a symmetric matrix in terms of which the uncertainties can be computed by use of the recursive formulae

$$\left.\begin{aligned} \overline{\overline{\mathbf{W}}}(1, 1) &= \overline{\overline{\sigma}} , \\ \overline{\overline{\mathbf{W}}}(k+1, k+1) &= \mathbf{A}\overline{\overline{\mathbf{W}}}(k, k)\mathbf{A}^{\mathrm{T}} + \overline{\overline{\mathbf{W}}}(1, 1) . \end{aligned}\right\} \tag{14}$$

In formulae (14) σ denotes the innovations covariance matrix defined in equation (4) and T is the transpose operator. Detailed derivations of the recursive formulae presented in equations (10) and (14) are available on request.

The covariance matrix σ is computed by use of the formula

$$\sigma_{ij} = R_{ij} S_i S_j \,, \tag{15}$$

where R_{ij} is the (i, j) entry in the Pearson correlation matrix for the regression residuals and S_j is the standard error of the regression for process X_j.

The k-steps-ahead forecasts for the integrated series $\hat{\overline{X}}^s(k)$ is obtained by direct summation:

$$\hat{\overline{X}}^s(k) = \overline{X}^s(0) + \sum_{n=1}^{k} \hat{\overline{X}}(n) \,. \tag{16}$$

The uncertainty of the deviation of $\hat{\overline{X}}^s(k)$ is now the variance of the sum of the deviations, $\overline{D}^s(k)$, and has the following recursive representation:

$$\mathrm{var}[\overline{D}^s(k)] = \mathrm{var}[\overline{D}^s(k-1)] + \overline{\overline{W}}(k, k) + 2 \sum_{n=1}^{k-1} \overline{\overline{W}}(n, k) \,. \tag{17}$$

4 A case study: Walsall 1952–1975
4.1 Identification
The results of the regression analysis for each of the twenty-two component processes is presented in table 2. The model parameters that differ from zero at the 1% level of significance are arranged according to the length-of-time lag, n, where the value of the maximum lag, N, is preset at three years. The critical value for the F statistic for 1% significance was $8 \cdot 1$. The column 'Min F' shows the value of the F statistic for the least significant effect included in the estimated equation. The column 'DW' shows the value of the Durbin–Watson statistic, measuring autocorrelation in the residuals to the regression equations and providing a partial test of the completeness of the specification, as required by equation (3). The critical values for DW at the 1% level are $1 \cdot 15$ for positive autocorrelation and $2 \cdot 85$ for negative autocorrelation. A value for DW outside this range is likely to indicate missing explanatory variables. R^2 is the coefficient of multiple correlation.

All of the estimated equations seem to be satisfactory according to these criteria. However, a detailed inspection of the time series revealed one component whose effects might be regarded as spurious. This was the chemicals group, B7, which is the smallest industrial group in Walsall with typically about 300 employees in total. In 1972 there were more than twice as many employees in this group as in the subsequent year and twice as many as in the previous year. This erratic behaviour can be

Table 2. Regression analysis.

Effects	R^2	DW	Min$F$	Constant	Causes		
					$n=1$	$n=2$	$n=3$
M	0·810	1·26	17·2	5137			+0·492M −2·276N
U	0·784	2·32	9·7	86	−1·021C		+1·216F
N	0·769	1·45	59·9	144	+0·928N		
A	0·633	1·54	9·3	−497		+1·539H	+0·770I
B1	0			−164			
B2	0·628	1·72	13·9	58		−1·829G	+0·291M
B3	0·599	1·72	11·3	149	−0·349B2 −0·564B4		
¶ B4	0·933	1·72	11·9	−191	+1·753B7	+7·354B7	−0·609B3 −0·66B8 +0·750C
¶ B5	0·678	2·04	9·4	273	−4·970B6		−11·455B7
B6	0·656	2·12	11·2	−55	+0·058B2	+0·223H	
B7	0·309	2·46	8·1	−10			+0·727B2
¶ B8	0·796	1·78	8·2	−73	+0·397C +0·397H	+1·404B7	
C	0			28			
D	0·754	2·29	13·9	−5		+0·266A	+0·267B3
E	0			172			
F	0·389	1·72	11·5	168			−0·395C
G	0·571	2·25	8·2	84	+0·228B1 −0·106E_F		
H	0			19			
I	0			276			
¶ E_M	0·610	1·91	10·7	326		+1·998B3	−19·218B7
¶ E_F	0·799	1·77	15·6	830			−19·449B7 +2·964G
¶ E_T	0·552	2·44	22·2	1547			−33·932B7

Table 3. Supplementary analysis.

Effects	R^2	DW	Min$F$	Constant	Causes		
					$n=1$	$n=2$	$n=3$
B4	0·828	2·22	9·8	−281	+1·066I	+0·191E_M	−0·273B1 −1·553E
B5	0			102			
B8	0·534	2·13	20·6	−48	+0·496C		
E_M	0			161			
E_F	0·448	1·53	14·6	486			−1·764C
E_T	0			473			

Table 4. Innovations correlation matrix.

	M	U	N	A	B1	B2	B3	B4	B5	B6	B7	B8	C	D	E	F	G	H	I	E_M	E_F	E_T
M	1																					
U		1																				
N		0·5741	1																			
A			0·5189	1																		
B1				0·3784	1																	
B2	-0·5193					1																
B3							1															
B4							0·3874	1														
B5		-0·3852	0·4510	-0·4540					1													
B6		0·5251		0·6348						1												
B7								-0·5019			1											
B8												1										
C	-0·4773												1									
D		-0·4278	-0·5863											1								
E									0·7032	-0·3877				0·5431	1							
F		-0·3889													0·5369	1						
G									0·5526								1					
H																		1				
I																			1			
E_M		0·5911	0·5837						0·7095						0·4413		0·4016	0·5121		1		
E_F	-0·5279	0·5548	-0·5278	0·3985					0·7934	-0·3901					0·6242		0·3992			0·5749	1	
E_T		0·4813	0·4878						0·8770						0·6479		0·5209			0·9391	0·7059	1

traced to a single minimum list heading[1] in one of the constituent employment-exchange areas which itself had over 300 employees in the year 1972 but none in previous or subsequent years. Industry B7 appears in components B4, B5, B8, E_M, E_F, and E_T indicated by the symbol ¶. A supplementary set of regressions were conducted for these six components in which group B7 was excluded. The results of these supplementary analyses are presented in table 3.

The innovations correlation matrix for the revised regression equations is given in table 4. Only entries that are significant at the 5% level are included.

4.2 Structure

The overall qualitative structure of the identified causal system can be presented in the form of a directed graph or *digraph* (Harary et al, 1965). If each component process is a vertex and each causal relation a directed edge, the digraph for table 2 contains the two cycles

$$
B3 \rightleftarrows B4 \qquad \text{and} \qquad
\begin{array}{ccc}
B2 & \longleftarrow & G \\
\downarrow & & \uparrow \\
B7 & \longrightarrow & E_F
\end{array}
.
$$

When the component B7 is deleted from the system both of these cycles are removed, the regression equation for B4 in the supplementary analysis no longer containing B3. The full causal structure is shown in figure 2. A digraph with no cycles admits a level assignment of vertices such that directed edges always end at higher-level numbers than those at which they commence (Harary et al, 1965, theorem 10.1). This theorem can be applied to extend our notion of basic activities to acyclic structures. A level number of unity is assigned to activities that are not caused by other activities in the system. These define the basic (level 1) activities in the sense used in the introduction of this paper. A level number of two is assigned to activities which are only affected by basic activities. In general an activity is assigned a level number of $L+1$ if it is affected by some activity of level L but by no activity with a level number exceeding L. According to this scheme the level assignment in table 5 is obtained.

There is a unique path of maximum length in the digraph which links all six levels:

$$
C \xrightarrow{\;-\;} E_F \xrightarrow{\;-\;} G \xrightarrow{\;-\;} B2 \xrightarrow{\;-\;} B3 \xrightarrow{\;+\;} D .
$$

It is interesting to note that this path begins and ends with service industries and passes through two industrial groups within the manufacturing sector. The stimulation of employment in the construction sector (C), as well as having the direct and indirect effects indicated in this path, directly

[1] Minimum list headings are subdivisions of the industrial orders in the Standard Industrial Classifications.

retards the expansion in unemployment. The stimulation of construction employment also depresses employment in miscellaneous services (F), which has the indirect effect of a further inhibition of the rise in unemployment.

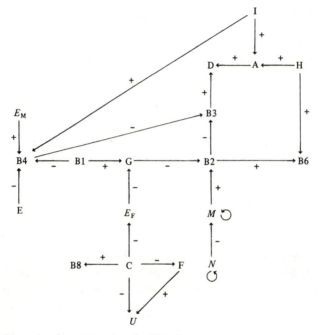

Figure 2. Causal structure for Walsall.

Table 5. The level assignment.

Level	Activities	Level	Activities
1	B1, B5, C, E, H, I, N, E_M, E_T	4	B2
2	A, B4, B8, F, M, E_F	5	B3, B6
3	G, U	6	D

4.3 Forecasts

Table 6 shows the results of the forecasts for each of the years 1976 to 1980. The column labelled X gives the forecast and W its standard deviation. E_T^A gives an alternative forecast for total employment obtained by aggregating the forecasts for the industrial groups. For 1976 this is 10095 jobs below the direct forecast. This corresponds to a discrepancy of 3·9 times the standard deviation of the direct forecast. This discrepancy seems to be attributable to the presence of the possibly spurious effect of the chemicals industry (B7) in the direct forecast for total employment.

In table 7 forecasts for 1976 are shown based on the supplementary analysis conducted for the six components which were affected by sector B7. The discrepancy between the direct and aggregated forecasts is reduced to 1248, well within the revised standard deviation of 3879. These two estimates of the 1976 expansion in employment (−775 and 473) are in strong disagreement with the original direct forecast of 14814. A choice of the most acceptable forecasting equation for total employment changes clearly needs to be made. The 1976 outturns for these changes can help us in this choice.

Before the forecasts are compared with the actual changes that occurred, it is instructive to review the full extent of the disagreements between the original and supplementary forecasts. The ratio of the absolute difference between the forecasts to the standard deviation of the supplementary forecast is calculated to give the following statistics (denoted by $|t|$):

B4: $3 \cdot 5^*$;   B5: $3 \cdot 3^*$;   B8: $0 \cdot 3$; E_M: $3 \cdot 4^*$; E_F: $6 \cdot 8^*$; E_T: $3 \cdot 7^*$.

Table 6. Original forecasts, 1976.

	X	W		X	W		X	W
A	−470	541	C	28	693	M	990	920
B1	−164	982	D	202	109	U	1352	523
B2	549	548	E	172	451	N	834	338
B3	893	396	F	10	334			
¶ B4	−1440	206	G	426	210	¶ E_M	8464	1539
¶ B5	4662	779	H	19	398	¶ E_F	8854	798
B6	−216	68	I	276	618	¶ E_T	14814	2597
B7	−10	128						
¶ B8	−218	212				¶ E_T^A	4719	

Table 7. Supplementary forecasts, 1976.

	X	W		X	W		X	W
B4	−2443	284	E_M	161	2464	E_T^A	−775	
B5	102	1371	E_F	−218	1321			
B8	−149	321	E_T	473	3879			

Table 8. Comparisons between the outturns and the initial and supplementary forecasts.

	Initial	Supplementary	Outturn
B4	−1440 ± 206	−2443 ± 284	−770
B5	4662 ± 779	102 ± 1371	−149
E_M	8464 ± 1539	161 ± 2464	2465
E_F	8854 ± 798	−218 ± 1321	4052
E_T	14814 ± 2597	473 ± 3879	6517

Table 9. Revised forecasts for 1976–1980: outturns for 1976 and updating for 1977–1980.

Process		1976 X	1976 W	1977 X	1977 W	1978 X	1978 W	1979 X	1979 W	1980 X	1980 W
M	a	990	920	2133	920	2935	920	3728	1282	4099	1467
	b	−3064		2133	924	2935	924	2566	924	4873	1286
U	a	1352	523	521	880	−682	880	70	969	598	969
	b	2467		−179	525	−682	880	1442	882	598	971
N	a	834	338	917	461	995	545	1068	608	1135	658
	b	467		577	339	487	462	496	546	504	610
A	a	−470	541	−1296	543	−898	817	−255	946	−255	946
	b	14		−1296	543	−315	543	2813	819	−255	948
B1	a	−164	982	−164	982	−164	982	−164	982	−164	982
	b	−637		−164	984	−164	984	−164	984	−164	984
B2	a	549	548	694	548	−1024	669	219	818	926	818
	b	−159		694	550	−1520	550	59	672	926	821
B3	a	893	396	1336	469	31	598	−127	646	173	782
	b	266		639	397	−2364	471	−202	600	674	648
B4	a	−2443	284	−220	719	1124	860	−178	1141	−178	1141
	b	−770		4024	292	1564	721	−967	861	−178	1143
B5	a	102	1371	102	1371	102	1371	102	1371	102	1371
	b	−149		102	1373	102	1373	102	1373	102	1373
B6	a	−216	68	−77	75	−11	116	−110	118	−38	121
	b	3		−118	69	74	76	−139	116	−47	119
B7	a	−10	128	−10	128	−10	128	−10	128	−10	128
	b	23		−10	128	−10	128	−10	128	−10	128
B8	a	−149	321	−34	470	−34	470	−34	470	−34	470
	b	−56		−306	322	−34	470	−34	470	−34	470
C	a	28	693	28	693	28	693	28	693	28	693
	b	713		28	693	28	693	28	693	28	693
D	a	202	109	50	109	−265	180	−165	198	32	262
	b	4		50	109	−136	109	−294	181	43	199
E	a	172	451	172	451	172	451	172	451	172	451
	b	763		172	452	172	452	172	452	172	452
F	a	10	334	444	334	248	334	157	432	157	433
	b	1139		444	335	248	335	−114	335	157	433
G	a	426	210	70	298	−135	298	−42	298	1	298
	b	697		−488	211	−135	299	−42	299	128	299
H	a	19	398	19	398	19	398	19	398	19	398
	b	398		19	398	19	398	19	398	19	398
I	a	276	618	276	618	276	618	276	618	276	618
	b	4258		276	618	276	618	276	618	276	618
E_M	a	161	2464	161	2464	161	2464	161	2464	161	2464
	b	2465		161	2464	161	2464	161	2464	161	2464
E_F	a	−218	1321	1721	1324	844	1324	437	1803	437	1803
	b	4052		1721	1324	844	1324	−772	1324	437	1803
E_T	a	473	3879	473	3879	473	3879	473	3879	473	3879
	b	6517		473	3879	473	3879	473	3879	473	3879

Since the critical value for this statistic at the 1% level for a normal distribution is $2 \cdot 7$, the asterisks indicate a significant difference between the forecasts for B4, B5, E_M, E_F, and E_T. The 1976 outturns thus provide five comparative tests for deciding between the original and supplementary forecasts, as indicated in table 8.

For sector B6 the initial forecast was clearly unrealistic whereas the supplementary forecast was confirmed. For male, female, and total employment the outturn was between the initial and supplementary forecasts but was closer to the supplementary forecast both absolutely and as a proportion of the appropriate standard deviations. For sector B4 the initial forecast was closer to the outturn than the supplementary forecast, but both forecasts were significant underestimates. The overall reliability of the 1976 forecasts thus does not seem to be seriously impaired by the exclusion of industry group B7 and we conclude that its effects are spurious.

The original model was therefore revised to incorporate the supplementary regression equations. The full set of forecasts obtained from the revised model for the years 1976 through to 1980 are given in table 9 in the rows marked 'a'.

4.4 Innovations

The full set of 1976 outturns is given in table 10. Column X shows the change that actually occurred in 1976. Column $|t|$ measures the significance of the differences between these changes and the corrected forecasts. At the 1% level the components B4, B6, F, I, M, and E_F exhibited significantly large innovations, and at the 5% level the component U did. Of these, table 4 showed correlations between B6, E_F, and U. Whereas the correlation between U and B6 was positive, those between E_F and B6 and between E_F and U were negative, indicative of an unusual direction for the 1976 innovation in E_F. The magnitude of the seven

Table 10. 1976 outturns.

Process	X	$|t|$	Process	X	$|t|$	Process	X	$|t|$
A	14	0·9	C	713	1·0	M	−3064	4·4*
B1	−637	0·5	D	4	1·8	U	2467	2·1**
B2	−159	1·3	E	763	1·3	N	467	1·1
B3	266	1·6	F	1139	3·4*	E_M	2465	0·9
B4	−770	5·9*	G	697	1·3	E_F	4052	3·2*
B5	−149	0·3	H	398	1·0	E_T	6517	1·6
B6	3	2·7*	I	4258	6·4*			
B7	23	0·3						
B8	−56	0·4						

* Significant at the 1% level.   ** Significant at the 5% level.

significant innovations in the Walsall system for 1976 are as follows:

B4: +1673   F: +1129 M: −4054 E_F: +4270
B6: +219   I: +3982 U: +1115 .

The updating of the Walsall forecasts to incorporate the effects of the 1976 innovations, by use of the current model form, is shown in table 9 in the rows marked 'b', the column for 1976 containing the outturns.

The results mark the completion of the first phase of the forecasting cycle. The next steps involve the estimation of new regression equations that use the 1976 outturns as part of the data base and their application to the calculation of new forecasts for the years 1977 through to 1981.

5 Conclusion
In conclusion we shall review four issues which we have helped to resolve by the case study reported in this paper.

1. To what extent does the causal structure of the Lowry model and the basic-sector/service-sector distinction provide a realistic model of the Walsall economy? It seems that the postwar development of industry in Walsall has followed a path which diverges considerably from that implicit in the Lowry model. Of six industrial groups that appear as basic sectors (level 1 in table 5), four industries, construction, distribution, transport, and the insurance/professional/scientific complex, are within the service category. None of these six industrial groups have effects on the growth of population in Walsall, and the growth of population is also not affected by the growth of the nonbasic industrial groups.

2. To what extent do the service sector, migration, and female employment act as regulators of unemployment? For the postwar Walsall economy it was found that the construction industry plays a crucial and positive role, and miscellaneous services a subsidiary and negative role. The stimulation of the local construction industry has appreciable direct and indirect effects in stemming the growth of unemployment in Walsall. Neither the level of female employment nor migration have direct detectable effects on unemployment in Walsall.

3. To what extent does the travel-to-work-area design prove suitable for local employment forecasting? Since no response of migration to local employment changes has been detected in Walsall, we must be circumspect about the extent to which Walsall is self-contained with respect to the supply of labour and can consider the possibilities that local changes in labour demand could be met either by changes in commuting into the area or by changes in the utilisation of local labour. The expansion of unemployment and female employment in response to contractions in the construction industry reinforce the hypothesis of local labour utilisation.

Such an effect helps to explain the nonresponse of the migration component in a manner that does not undermine the viability of the travel-to-work-area design.

4. To what extent can local Department of Employment data be used for producing employment forecasts at a fine level of disaggregation? In our case study the chemical-industry series was removed from the analysis because of a data anomaly. This indicates a general need for caution when small sectors are being used to predict changes in other sectors. Under these circumstances a careful inspection of the employment time series needs to be conducted prior to their use in the regression model. Anomalous series would need to be deleted, combined with other sectors, or prefiltered, possibly with the use of dummy variables.

An alternative approach, suggested by Allen and Yuill (1978), would involve the use of plant-level information, but it could be some time yet before such sources provide good enough series for forecasting purposes.

References
Allen K, Yuill D, 1978 *Small Area Employment Forecasting* (Saxon House, Teakfield, Farnborough, Hants)
Ball R J, 1978 *Committee on Policy Optimisation Report* Cmnd 7148 (HMSO, London)
Barras R, Broadbent T A, Cordey-Hayes M, Massey D B, Robinson K, Willis J, 1971 "An operational urban development model of Cheshire" *Environment and Planning* 3 115-234
Batty M, 1976 *Urban Modelling: Algorithms, Calibrations and Predictions* (Cambridge University Press, London)
Brown A J, 1972 *The Framework of Regional Economics in the United Kingdom* (National Institute for Economic and Social Research, London; Cambridge University Press, London)
Caines P E, 1976 "Weak and strong feedback free processes" *IEEE Transactions on Automatic Control* 21 737-739
Caines P E, Chan C W, 1975a "Feedback between stationary stochastic processes" *IEEE Transactions on Automatic Control* 20 498-508
Caines P E, Chan C W, 1975b "Estimation, identification and feedback" in *System Identification: Advances and Case Studies* Eds D G Lainiotis, R V Mehra (Academic Press, New York) pp 349-405
Caines P E, Sethi S D, 1977 "Recursiveness, causality and feedback" Division of Engineering and Applied Physics, Harvard University, Cambridge, Mass (mimeo)
Department of Employment, 1965 "Key to industry code letters" HQW 610-100 5/65 EC, Department of Employment, London
Department of Employment, 1970 "Review of travel to work areas" *Department of Employment Gazette* 77(9) 778-779
Department of Employment, 1972 "Comparison between the 1968 and 1958 Standard Industrial Classifications" HQW 529-200 10/72 PB, Department of Employment, London
Drewett R, Connock C, Goddart J, Pinkham R, Spence N, 1974 "Urban change in Britain: 1961-1971 Standard Metropolitan Labour Areas and Metropolitan Economic Labour Areas" Working Reports 1 and 2, Department of Geography, London School of Economic and Political Science, London

Eversley D E C, 1965 "Population economy and society" in *Population in History* Eds R V Glass, D E C Eversley (Edward Arnold, London) pp 23-69

Fielding A J, 1971 "Internal migration in England and Wales" UWP-14, Centre for Environmental Studies, London

Granger C W J, 1969 "Investigating causal relations by econometric models and cross-spectral methods" *Econometrica* **37** 424-438

Harary F, Norman R, Cartwright D, 1965 *Structural Models: An Introduction to the Theory of Directed Graphs* (John Wiley, Chichester, Sussex)

Hyman G, 1977 "Causal determination" WN-448, Centre for Environmental Studies, London

Hyman G, 1978 "How to improve local population estimates" *CES Review* **4** 60-61

Hyman G, Booth D, 1978a "A comparative study of the post-war development of the U.K. and Soviet manufacturing sectors" WN-478, Centre for Environmental Studies, London; to be published in *Sovietology in Reverse: The Lessons of East European Experience* Eds S Markowski, R Portes (Macmillan, London)

Hyman G, Booth D, 1978b "The analysis of local demographic and employment changes in the West Midlands (I)" WN-476, Centre for Environmental Studies, London

Hyman G, Palmer D J, 1978 "A regional analysis of the dependency between registered unemployment and the stocks and flows of notified vacancies" *Environment and Planning A* **10** 853-866

Lowry I S, 1964 *A Model of Metropolis* RM-4125-RC, The Rand Corporation, Santa Monica, Calif.

Nie N H, Hull C H, Jenkins J G, Steinbrenner K, Bent D H, 1975 *Statistical Package for the Social Sciences* 2nd edition (McGraw-Hill, New York)

Pierce D A, Hough L D, 1977 "Causality in temporal systems: characterisations and a survey" *Journal of Econometrics* **5** 265-293

Sayer R A, 1976 *Progress in Planning, Volume 6, Part 3. A Critique of Urban Modelling* (Pergamon Press, Oxford)

Sims C A, 1972 "Money, income, and causality" *American Economic Review* **62** 590-552

Smart M, 1974 *Progress in Planning, Volume 2, Part 4. Labour Market Areas: Uses and Definition* (Pergamon Press, Oxford)

Shenfield M I, 1967 "A comparison of the Standard Industrial Classification 1948 with the revised Classification for 1958" Department of Employment, London (mimeo)

Externalities for Manufacturing Industry in British Subregions

P M TOWNROE
University of East Anglia

"Agglomeration economies, external economies of scale and indivisibilities are crucial elements in regional and urban growth, especially spatial externalities and urbanisation economies ... . It is relatively easy to accommodate agglomeration economies in a model in a generalised way. What is difficult is that when we come to operationalise the model we have as yet made little headway in how to measure, even how to define, these agglomeration economies" (Richardson, 1973, pages 209-210).

1 Introduction

The notion of agglomeration economies is a central concept in regional economics, felt by many to lie at the heart of the spatial-economic theory of the firm as well as urban and regional growth theory. Agglomeration economies are, however, notoriously difficult to identify and quantify. The evidence on their present importance to manufacturing industry in the United Kingdom has therefore been unclear and somewhat ambivalent. Many studies have focussed on local interindustrial linkages as the most direct evidence of agglomeration economies but the results of these studies fail to show whether such local linkages are significant to the performance of firms in an area, or whether other elements of agglomeration economies are important also.

This paper presents some early results from an attempt to use a unique data set from the 1968 UK Census of Production to see if it is possible to identify the impact of different aspects of agglomeration economies on the performance of individual industrial sectors measured by net output per head. The analysis uses data for the sixty-one subregions of Great Britain for a total of fifty-three sectors in manufacturing industry. In particular, this data set allows a number of calculations undertaken by Brown (1972, chapter 7) for 1948 and 1954, to test the influence of agglomeration economies, to be repeated for 1968 at a finer level of disaggregation, both by region and by industrial sector. The next section of the paper briefly discusses the nature of agglomeration economies. Section 3 characterises recent empirical work on linkages and external economies; section 4 describes the three dependent variables used in the analysis; section 5 lists and describes the agglomeration variables; section 6 presents some preliminary results before a number of conclusions are offered in section 7.

2 The nature of agglomeration economies

Agglomeration economies have traditionally been divided into internal economies of scale, localisation economies, and urbanisation economies.

A fourth category, transfer economies due to physical proximity, has also sometimes been proposed, although this may be seen as one aspect of urbanisation economies. The concept may be applied to the welfare of individual consumers but is more usually discussed in terms of industrial enterprises and individual industrial plants or establishments.

For the analysis which follows, the three-fold distinction for economies in production is important. Internal economies of scale for a firm may arise in managerial, marketing, research, or financial functions and may not necessarily result in spatial concentration at one location. But internal economies, usually more obviously technological, will also arise at the level of the individual establishments with increasing size. If the size of the establishments in an individual industry varies by region, the influence of the economies of scale so implied will need to be taken account of before other (external) influences contributing to differences in performance can be explained.

Economies of localisation are economies external to the firm but internal to the industry. They arise when plants of a complementary or related range of industries or with a similar range of products aggregate in one area. The benefits available to firms under this heading will include access to a pool of labour with skills appropriate to the processes of the industry, the availability of specialised services, and a concentration of suppliers and customers. Urbanisation economies, the third category of agglomeration economy, are closely related to economies of localisation but are more general, not being specific to a single industry but occurring whenever a large number of industrial plants congregate together. They include common facilities such as commerce and banking, technical servicing, education, and general subcontracting as well as a large general (and perhaps skilled and adaptable) labour pool. Both forms of agglomeration economy yield a comparative advantage to plants which arises from spatial concentration.

The spatial distribution of industry does of course reflect a high degree of historical inertia. The locational advantages which lead to a plant being established on a given site may subsequently change but the management of the firm owning the plant does not necessarily respond quickly to the new pattern of locational advantage. There is a learning lag. For a change of location to be induced, the pattern of costs has to have altered by a margin large enough to cover, on a discounted basis, the cost of upheaval and relocation. The limited differences in operating costs in different locations in a spatially compact, highly urbanised economy such as that of the United Kingdom therefore suggest that locational redistribution has usually to wait for the full stimulus of growth or the more limited push stimuli of compulsory purchase orders, etc, rather than to act upon changing agglomeration economies alone.

The response to change in local circumstances of an industrial plant will be even more tardy if the owners or managers are not profit maximisers or if there is considerable uncertainty about the future of the firm or of the pattern of locational advantage. Evidence of comparative advantage arising from agglomeration economies is therefore difficult to deduce from the spatial distribution of plants alone.

A further problem in identifying the *benefits* to plants of spatial propinquity is that there will also be *costs* from the same source. The cost of labour may be higher in the larger urban areas (although unit labour costs may be lower owing to higher productivity). Taxes may be higher, as well as the cost of industrial floorspace. Even transport costs, owing to local congestion, may be higher in city centres than for plants located close to a motorway system outside or on the edge of the urban area. Urbanisation economies have both positive and negative components, which vary sector by sector.

The importance of agglomeration economies to an individual firm, depending upon the product and the process, may well also vary with the stage in the life of the company, and/or the size of the company, and/or the stage in the life of the specific product or process. Therefore within a given industrial sector there will be new concerns, small concerns, and plants developing a new product or process for all of which there will be a need to keep capital overheads down, to maintain maximum flexibility in the face of swiftly developing experience, to keep in close touch with suppliers and customers, and to use to the full the services only found in larger urban areas. Plants with these characteristics but without access to the economies of localisation and urbanisation may find it difficult to survive in the face of competition from plants with these advantages.

Without examining the issue at length we might argue that agglomeration economies in general, and local interindustry linkages in particular, will be more important for small undercapitalised owner-managed firms, for plants in which the process has to be speedily adaptable and sensitive to technological change, and for processes which produce nonuniform and custom-built goods and which are fairly specialised by skill rather than by the capital equipment involved. If restrictions on entry to a sector are few and the capital requirements are low, agglomeration economies permit a given sector to achieve a high birthrate of new units. If the converse of these various propositions holds true, then in many sectors of manufacturing we must expect not to find evidence of the importance of agglomeration economies. Or perhaps only evidence of the importance of particular kinds of agglomeration economy. This will be important in evaluating the results which follow.

3 Past empirical work
Past empirical studies on agglomeration economies and local linkages can be classified into four groups. In this section these groups are characterised in order to place the present work into context; but this characterisation in no way represents an attempt to review systematically the very large number of studies in this area.

3.1 Aggregate studies

It is possible to argue that a strong concentration of industry in a single area or a close spatial association between industrial sectors suggests either a functional interdependency between the plants (that is, strong local interfirm linkages) or a mutual benefit from a general external economy (such as the labour pool or common services). Studies such as those of Richter (1969) in the United States, of Streit (1969) in France and West Germany, and of Lever (1972) in the United Kingdom have found distinctive spatial associations between pairs and groups of industries. However, if historical inertia is strong, mere spatial association can be no sure indicator of continuing intersectoral spatial interdependence or of the presence of currently significant agglomeration economies. [Although Lever (1972) strengthens his analysis by relating the spatial patterning of industrial sectors to the functional linkages seen in the national input–output table.]

3.2 Cross-sectional surveys

Although inertia may mean that a firm continues to have links with other firms which do not reflect full economic efficiency, either for that firm or for a modern best-practice plant with the same product, an obvious way to assess the importance of local linkages is to question industrial plants directly on the pattern of their sales and purchases. Keeble's (1969) study of 124 plants in northwest London is an example of such a survey; or the survey by Economic Consultants Ltd (1971) of 1434 plants located in southeast England. These surveys distinguish linkage economies from other external economies and they have found that linkages typically extend over wide geographical areas for most industrial firms. Only among small firms in engineering and metal fabricating are local linkages predominant, perhaps because these firms are themselves providing something of a local service to other firms. The very detailed study of twenty-four companies in Scotland by Lever (1974) reinforces this conclusion.

3.3 External economies for new investments

If any study which includes older plants is weakened by identifying linkages or locational patterns which reflect past locational choices and a degree of managerial inertia, then an obvious further approach is to consider the location of new investment in order to try to identify whether agglomeration economies play a role in locational choice. This consideration may be on the basis of aggregate data, looking at spatial patterns of investment or employment or output growth. The analyses of Keeble and Hauser in the United Kingdom (1971 and 1972) or of Wheat (1973), Harris and Hopkins (1972), and Richardson (1974) in the United States all use correlation and regression analysis and a variety of proxy indicators for agglomeration economies. Their results suggest that such economies are important but are subsidiary to other factors (from government grants to climate and market accessibility) encouraging industrial growth.

Alternatively, the role of agglomeration economies in locational choice may be identified directly from questions to managers in recently established plants. By far the most comprehensive British survey is that undertaken by the British government (Department of Trade and Industry, 1973)—the 'ILAG' survey—of 543 plants being newly established between 1964 and 1967. This survey showed that "Access to supplies of raw materials or components" was a major locational factor for 15% of cases and a minor factor for a further 14%. A question was not asked on access to local markets, although access to markets in general was a major factor for 30% of cases and a minor factor for 14%. "Availability of industrial and commercial services" was a major factor for only 3% and a minor factor for 5%. The dominant locational factor overall (major factor for 72%) was the availability of labour.

A further way to attack the importance of local linkages for new plants directly is to pose questions about the pattern of ties with suppliers and customers after a new plant has opened. Moseley and Townroe (1973) for example reported on two surveys which revealed the general unimportance of local linkages for plants in their new site except for a subgroup of engineering firms involved in nonroutine or batch production of a changing product range, and which suffered a forced move (lease fell in, compulsory purchase order, etc). In the ILAG survey only 19% of the mobile firms were not relying on the same sources of materials and components at the new location as at the old. And only 24% obtained more than half their supplies from within forty miles. However 37% put out subcontract work to firms within forty miles.

3.4 Productivity and external economies

Brown (1972) used values of net output per head by industrial Standard Order for twelve regions in Great Britain in 1948 and 1954 to test whether the growth or the level of productivity is associated with the size of agglomerations of an industry. Working with industrial cross sections, he found no general association between the size of an industry in a region and a high growth rate of per capita output; or again no association when all industries were taken together. Using the level of net output per head, and allowing for regional differences in average plant size, even though for the majority of industries this was not significant, he found the employment in an industry in a region to be positively and significantly associated only in clothing, leather and fur, wood and cork, and in all trades together. Regional dummies were significant when all industries were taken together for the London and West Midlands conurbations, the South and the East regions, and the North Midlands.

This present study is a development of Brown's work, and is an attempt to see if agglomeration economies influence the performance of individual industrial sectors, measured by an (imperfect) productivity ratio. It was prompted in particular by a study of regional differences in industrial

productivity in Mexico by Laos (1977) which found clear evidence of the
importance of agglomeration economies, and also by the work of Aberg
(1973) on productivity in Swedish manufacturing which found higher
productivity in the more populous and the more densely settled regions,
both size of enterprise and capital intensity having been standardised.
Like that of Brown (and those of Laos and Aberg) this study takes out
the effect of internal scale economies before examining the influence of a
number of proxy variables for agglomeration economies on the productivity
ratio. Unlike the earlier approaches to the identification of agglomeration
economies, the use of direct performance measures avoids the difficulties
posed by historical inertia, by attributing importance to identified local
linkages, and by estimates provided to questionnaire surveys. But the
cross-sectional analysis used here is not without its own difficulties as we
shall see.

4 The dependent variables

Following Brown, the first dependent variable used is the value of net
output per head by product group and subregion from the 1968 UK
Census of Production. Values of this variable (Y_1) have been provided by
special tabulations from the Business Statistics Office (BSO) for each of
the Census product groups 4 to 86 (those covering manufacturing industry)
and for the sixty-one subregions of Great Britain and the eleven economic
planning regions of the United Kingdom. [The regions and subregions are
defined in HMSO (1969). The product groups are defined in terms of the
minimum list headings of the 1968 Standard Industrial Classification (SIC)
in the appendix to HMSO (1974).] The data set is not complete for not
only is each product group not represented in every region but in some
regions the figures have been suppressed because the number of returns is so
small that there is a risk of disclosing information relating to an individual
enterprise[1]. For this paper, where information on a product group is
available only for fewer than fifteen subregions that group has been
excluded from the analysis. The fifty-three groups used in the analysis are
listed in table 2. Suppressed figures in certain subregions in the groups
which were used probably give the analysis of some of these groups a
small degree of urban and larger subregion bias.

The values of net output per head are an imperfect indicator of
productivity or performance. In many industries the variation in net

[1] A proportion of the figures are based upon the combined returns from firms who
did not respond to the Census with separate figures for each establishment. Estimates
were made by the BSO of the regional and subregional figures by a pro rata allocation
according to the number of operatives employed at each establishment. Further
estimates had then to be made to allow for small establishments employing fewer than
twenty-five persons that were not required to make detailed returns to the Census, and
for unsatisfactory returns for each industry at the national level. In some subregions
where there were only a few establishments employing fewer than twenty-five persons
each there was no satisfactory base for this estimation and the figures were suppressed.

output per head between establishments *within* a subregion is likely to be greater than the variation *between* subregions. Also net output, as defined by the BSO, is not quite the same thing as the more relevant concept for productivity measurement, namely value added. The value of services bought from other businesses and institutions which lie mainly outside manufacturing industry (including hire of plant and machinery, payments for repairs and maintenance, advertising and selling expenses) is included in net output but these services are normally excluded from the concept of value added. [The relevant definitions and the changing usages by the BSO have recently been clearly explained by the Chief Statistician (Mitchell, 1978).] Data on the value of these services are not available by sector and by subregion and so the net output measure used here cannot be modified.

Differences between subregions in the values of net output per head may come from a number of different sources. This analysis concentrates upon plant economies of scale and agglomeration economies. But low communication costs or low site costs could permit high earnings and/or high profits per employee. Within each industrial grouping the level of product competition might vary, allowing higher profits to firms in one or a number of regions. Or higher net output might reflect greater capital intensity prompted by cheaper or more available capital or by more expensive labour. Or higher product prices, leading to a higher net output figure, may be associated with dear labour. Since we know that the price of labour varies significantly by region in the United Kingdom, it would clearly be preferable to modify our original variable.

The special tabulations allow such a modification to be made. By providing a figure (by product group and subregion again) for wages and salaries as a percentage of net output, the tables allow the derivation of a figure of net output minus wages and salaries per employee (Y_2). This variable, with the caveats noted above, is essentially the income from capital per employee and is the second dependent variable.

Since in looking at productivity we are essentially interested in efficiency or output per unit of input, a desirable further dependent variable is one which reflects both the capital and the labour inputs. If the first two dependent variables are influenced by capital intensity, the only measure available to measure that intensity is that expressed as one minus wages and salaries as a percentage of net output, a measure of the return to capital. This measure of capital intensity can hardly be used as an independent variable (because of the high correlation with Y_1 and Y_2 implied by the definitions). No capital-stock figures are available at this level of disaggregation. So to reflect both labour and capital inputs we can use a modified version of a generalised efficiency index from Laos (1977). This index is a standard total-factor productivity index expressed in relative terms, comparing each subregion with the national average position.

In simplified notation the index π_i for a given industry in one subregion is

$$\pi_i = \frac{Q_i}{Q} \bigg/ \left(\alpha \frac{L_i}{L} + \beta \frac{K_i}{K} \right) ,$$

where Q_i, L_i, and K_i are the values of net output and the labour and capital input of the industry in subregion i, and Q, L, and K are the values for the industry nationally, while α and β are the national shares of labour and capital in income. The index therefore relates the net output in a subregion as a proportion of the national net output of the industry in question to the share of that subregion in the utilization of primary inputs in relation to the inputs used by the industry nationally. The average level of efficiency at the national level is obviously unity. A region has a higher than average (national) level of efficiency if $\pi_i > 1$ and vice versa if $\pi_i < 1$.

The assumptions behind the construction of this fairly general index are set out in Laos (1977, chapter 4). In order to be able to use it from the data available, dependent variable (Y_3) is a modification:

$$\pi_i = 1 \bigg/ \left(\alpha \frac{q}{q_i} + 1 - \alpha_i \right) ,$$

where α_i and α are the regional and national labour shares in net output and q_i and q are the regional and national values of net output per head for the industry. This derivation is set out in the appendix. It makes the assumption that the cost of capital is uniform across regions by industry, and it ignores quality differences in the inputs, referring only to the use made of the inputs.

A further potential indicator of performance, growth in employment in the subregion in each industry, was considered but not used. This is because variations in employment growth rates between subregions were clearly strongly influenced in 1968 by regional policy and the New and Expanding Towns programme as well as by differential investment rates, reflected in different levels of labour productivity. Growth in net output would have been more appropriate but these figures are not available.

5 The independent variables
Returning to the discussion of section 2 above we may think of potential independent variables reflecting agglomeration economies in three groups: internal economies of scale, economies of localisation, and urbanisation economies.

5.1 Internal economies of scale
Two potential variables are available, by product group and by subregion: net output per establishment and average number employed per establishment. The first produced more significant correlations with the dependent variables. It also makes more sense in terms of the scale

economies, especially if the prices of capital and labour are relatively fixed. After experimentation on the assumption that economies of scale are rarely linear, the *log of net output per establishment* was adopted (X_1).

5.2 Economies of localisation

It is difficult to identify unambiguously the source of those agglomeration economies which are specific to a particular industry. One possibility is the size of the pool of labour skills specific to that industry in the subregion. A weighted index could be prepared reflecting the skill mix used in the industry locally or on average nationally. Such an index would fail to reflect, however, the ease with which employees in certain occupation groups can transfer to other occupations. A further and similar possibility is an index of the nonindustrial services used by the industry. Unfortunately, the relevant detailed information is not available at the subregional level.

However, information is available, at the national level, of the pattern of purchases by each industrial sector from each other industrial sector. It has therefore been possible to construct an *index of potential local industrial input linkages* for each industry in each subregion, weighting the proportion of the purchases of industry j from industry i nationally by the size (numbers employed) of industry i in the subregion:

$$A_j^h = \sum_{j=1}^{M} \frac{X_i^h}{\sum\limits_{h=1}^{T} X_i^h} \, a_{ij} \, ,$$

where

A_j^h is the index of potential local interindustrial input linkages in industry j in subregion h;

a_{ij} is the national input–output coefficient of industry i in relation to industry j ($j = 1, ..., M$);

X_i^h is employment in industry i in subregion h;

$\sum\limits_{h=1}^{T} X_i^h$ is employment in industry i across all subregions ($h = 1, ..., T$).

Variable A_j^h cannot be calculated for all of the fifty-three product groups used in the analysis because of incompatible industrial classifications in the data sources[2]. The variable was constructed for an initial ten product groups. However, the correlations, in all ten groups, of this variable with the three dependent variables were so low that the variable was subsequently dropped from the analysis. Given the findings of the studies referred to

[2] The 1968 product groups bring together the minimum list headings of the 1968 SIC in a slightly different way than do the industrial groupings of the 1968 input– output tables (HMSO, 1973). The data on employment by industry by subregion were kindly provided by M Chisholm of the University of Cambridge. These are classified by the 1958 SIC (see Chisholm and Oeppen, 1973), and so have to be transformed where possible to the 1968 groupings.

earlier in the paper, it would perhaps have been surprising to have found strong correlations in all sectors. However, it was disappointing to find such low correlations in the ten sectors examined, in all of which there was a prima facie case to expect significant local input linkages. The industries examined were: pumps and valves, mechanical handling equipment, industrial plant, nonelectrical machinery, other mechanical engineering, scientific instruments, electrical machinery, radio and radar, engineers small tools, and hand tools and implements.

5.3 Urbanisation economies

Three variables, each reflecting a separate aspect of urbanisation economies, were initially adopted for the two regression models tested. Further variables were available. Each of these provided alternative proxy measures for the presence of urbanisation economies and were not included in the regression models on the basis of very low correlations with the dependent variables compared with the three alternatives which were used. Each of the variables considered is not specific to an industry but is general to the subregion and so may be seen as a subregional characteristic. [Five of the variables were taken from among those used by Sant (1975) in his analysis of industrial movement between subregions within Great Britain.]

The number of employees in manufacturing industry in the subregion (X_3)
This variable reflects the pool of labour in a subregion within which a manufacturing concern has to hunt for workers. Although there is clearly some transferability within and between occupations from construction, the utilities, and the services sectors, especially among white-collar grades[3], this variable does give a nonspecific indicator of the relative numbers of employees available, particularly in skilled and semiskilled grades.

The percentage unemployment rate, 1966–1970, average of June and December (X_4)
A large pool of unemployed labour may also act as a form of urbanisation economy to a firm in manufacturing industry. However, this variable, specified as a *rate* of unemployment, is taken as a proxy for a decaying industrial environment and an older capital stock, high unemployment rates being associated with areas of industrial decline. This was particularly true at the end of the 1960s in Great Britain when the national unemployment rate was very low. This variable is therefore expected to correlate negatively with productivity and efficiency.

---

[3] If the labour force in a given sector or in sectors in general has more administrative, technical, and clerical staff (ATCs) as a proportion of total employees in plants in more urban areas, and if these occupations are on average more highly paid than other grades, then clearly net output per head will rise in more urban areas, and labour productivity will need to be higher to maintain income from capital per head. However, across the fifty-four sectors correlations of ATCs as a percentage of the total labour force with the percentage of the region defined as urban was significant in only one industry: bricks and fireclay.

Percentage of subregion with urban status (X_5)

Urbanisation economies may be expected to be larger in those subregions which are more highly urbanised. This variable measures the proportion of each subregion which was defined as urban by its administrative status as a borough or urban district in 1968. This definition of course ignores the urban development in rural districts adjoining major urban centres; but the elements of the urban system contributing to urbanisation economies are more likely to be associated with the central urban areas.

The other variables examined as potential candidates for inclusion in the regression models included:

(1) the number of males and females in the total local labour force;
(2) the numbers of skilled and semiskilled in the total local labour force;
(3) the population of the subregion [suggested by both Baumol (1967) and Richardson (1973) as an appropriate proxy for a variety of agglomeration economies];
(4) the density of employment in the urban areas, reflecting potential access to agglomeration economies;
(5) the percentage of the region with urban status;
(6) the net migration from the subregion, high out-migration perhaps suggesting a lower quality of work force;
(7) the status of the subregion for the regional development policy of the central government, perhaps indicating need rather than potential for economies of urbanisation.

6 Some results

An important preliminary exercise in this analysis was to see if the average size of plant did in fact correlate in each industry with the productivity variables chosen, thereby suggesting economies of scale which should thereafter be partialled out when seeking the influence of other agglomeration variables. The significance of these correlations is summarised in table 1, with the use of the log of plant size (X_1), measured as net output per establishment.

The industries or product groups referred to in table 1 may be identified by the listing in table 2. Of the fifty-three industries, only three did not show the expected positive correlation for Y_1 and Y_2, and eight for Y_3. Only one industry—45, radio and radar—had negative and significant correlation coefficients. These results are in striking contrast to those of Brown (1972, page 153), for whom "... differences between regions in average plant size seem rarely to have significant effects on productivity". The correlations of table 1 have been taken as sufficiently strong to require the size-of-plant variable (X_1) to be forced into all regression models tested. As a first step in examining the agglomeration variables, two regression models were tested, both incorporating the size of plant (X_1) and the size of the manufacturing labour force in the subregion (X_3). The results for

the dependent variable, net output minus wages and salaries per head (Y_2),
are summarised in table 2.

Table 2 clearly suggests that variable X_3 is not a very satisfactory proxy
for agglomeration economies, acting either for these economies in general
or for the specific economy of a large local labour pool. The signs of the
coefficients are negative for eighteen industries, including a group of
industries in which a priori reasoning might have suggested important
agglomeration economies and hence positive coefficients (for example,
industries 38–41 and 46. These sectors, however, were all fast-growing in
the 1960s and therefore were strongly influenced by regional policy in the
location of new investment). The erratic sign in the constant also suggests
an underspecified equation. The size-of-plant variable (X_1) continues to
perform well, however, as in the correlations, being negative in only three
industries and nonsignificant in fourteen.

The same equation with net output per head (Y_1) as the dependent
variable gives very similar results to those shown in table 2. The size-of-
plant variable (X_1) is significant in all but ten industries and significant
and negative only in industry 45. But the size of the manufacturing
labour force (X_3) has a negative coefficient in thirteen sectors and is
positive and significant in only fifteen sectors. With the efficiency index
as dependent variable (Y_3), the picture changes somewhat as shown in
table 3. The constant term is significant at the 1% level in all fifty-three
sectors. The size-of-plant variable (X_1) is positive and significant in forty-
one sectors; and the manufacturing-labour-force variable was positive and
significant in thirty sectors. If we accept that the equation with the

Table 1. Significance of correlations between net output per establishment ($\log X_1$)
and three productivity variables (Y_1, Y_2, and Y_3) by product group.

Significance level	Net output per head (Y_1)	Net output minus wages and salaries per head (Y_2)	Index of efficiency (Y_3)
1%	4, 6, 8, 9, 11, 14, 26, 28, 34, 35, 37, 38, 45, 50, 64, 67, 68, 73, 74, 79, 80, 82, 83, 85	4, 5, 6, 11, 14, 28 34, 35, 37, 38, 41, 64, 68, 73, 74, 79, 82, 83, 85	4, 6, 8, 9, 14, 23, 25, 29, 37, 38, 45, 46, 50, 52–55, 59, 64, 67, 68 71, 73, 74, 78, 79, 80, 82, 83, 86
5%	5, 12, 23, 25, 29, 40 41, 63, 71, 78, 86	8, 9, 12, 23, 26, 40, 57, 61, 63, 67, 70, 80, 86	11, 12, 26, 27, 28, 30, 34, 48 and 49, 84, 85
10%	30, 52–55, 59, 61, 76, 84	25, 29, 45, 71	39, 41, 57
Not significant	27, 31, 39, 42, 46, 47, 48 and 49, 57, 69, 70, 72, 81	27, 30, 31, 39, 42, 46, 47, 48 and 49, 50, 52–55, 59, 69, 72, 76, 77, 81, 84	5, 31, 40, 42, 47, 61, 63, 69, 70, 72, 76, 81

efficiency index is less open to bias from omitted variables which relate to capital (for example, age of capital), then this index must reflect the influence of our agglomeration economies on plant performance more adequately than the two simpler net output variables. With the efficiency index, only in industry 45 is there a negative (but not significant) coefficient to X_3. This therefore suggests that the two Y_1 and Y_2 equations are in some way underspecified in respect of an aspect of capital, rather than that the negative signs seen for variable X_3 in table 2 suggest a switch between positive agglomeration economies and negative agglomeration economies for different sectors. This may be made clearer by extending the model to include other indicators of agglomerative advantage.

One of the interesting features of table 3 is the significance of the coefficients in the textiles, clothing, and footwear sectors and in timber, furniture, and paper. The significance of the coefficient for newspapers and publishing is perhaps to be expected, if it is remembered that the new technology of computer typesetting, etc had not then arrived. This technology has been introduced most rapidly among provincial newspapers, so the role of agglomeration economies in this sector may be diminishing. The significant positive coefficients in the bricks and glass sectors were a surprise but are explained by the refractory goods and china in the bricks sector and the manufacture of glass containers in the glass sector. The lack of significant coefficients in the engineering sectors may reflect the distribution of new investment in these sectors to the Assisted Areas and to the hinterlands surrounding the major conurbations.

The disappointing results with X_3 in many sectors in table 2 might be improved by trying additionally to take account of the extent to which each subregion is urbanised and of the age of the capital stock in a region. We have no information on the size or the age of capital stock by industry by subregion, but if we accept an essentially structural explanation for relatively high unemployment in industrially declining subregions (and accept that by 1968 regional policy had had a limited overall impact on this structure–unemployment linkage), then we might use the unemployment rate as a crude proxy for the vintage of capital overall in a subregion. We can then relate this imperfect variable (X_4) to the productivity of that capital by sector.

In table 4 the regression model is extended, and again Y_2 is used as the dependent variable. X_4 and X_5 are now included. The adjusted R^2 all increase, although some very marginally. The size-of-plant variable (X_1) is significant for thirty-six sectors and has a negative coefficient in only five sectors. The X_3 variable again has both positive and negative (seventeen sectors) coefficients and is positive and significant in only thirteen sectors. The unemployment-rate variable (X_4) has the expected negative sign in all but thirteen sectors and is both negative and significant in thirteen sectors. The sectors in which this variable has positive but not significant coefficients include many which are not or are only weakly represented in the

Table 2. Regression results for net output minus wages and salaries per head.

Product group	Number of regions	Constant	X_1	X_3	$\bar{R}^2$
4 Grain milling products	43	***	***	**	0·499
5 Bread, flour confectionery	49	***	***	–a	0·162
6 Bacon, meat, fish	40	–	***	–	0·144
8 Cocoa, chocolate confectionery	23		**		0·197
9 Fruit, vegetable products	26		**		0·146
11 All other food products	49	*|	***	–	0·231
12 Beer and malt	38		***	*|	0·110
14 Soft drinks, cider	42	***	***	**	0·558
23 Synthetic resins	19	–	*	–	0·082
25 Other chemicals	47		*	–	0·044
26 Iron and steel	38		**	*	0·088
27 Aluminium	17				–0·082
28 Copper, brass	27	**|	***	–	0·386
29 Agricultural machinery	21		*		0·045
30 Machine tools	26	*		*|	0·022
31 Pumps, valves	27	**			–0·068
34 Construction equipment	19	**|	***		0·301
35 Mechanical handling equipment	27	*|	***		0·317
37 Industrial plant	46	–	***	**	0·264
38 Nonelectrical machinery	42	*|	***	–	0·241
39 Other mechanical engineering	39	***		–	–0·034
40 Photographic equipment	24		**	–	0·058
41 Scientific instruments	30	–	***	–	0·181
42 Electrical machinery	29				0·003
45 Radio, radar	32	***	*|	*	0·062
46 Domestic electrical goods	15			–	–0·165
47 Miscellaneous electrical goods	29	**			–0·061

Table 3. Regression results for the efficiency index.

Product group	Number of regions	Constant	X_1	X_3	$\bar{R}^2$
4	43	***	***	***	0·361
5	49	***			–0·042
6	40	***	***	***	0·409
8	23	***	***	**	0·491
9	26	***	***	*	0·464
11	49	***	*		0·049
12	38	***		**	0·129
14	42	***		*	0·602
23	19	***	***		0·434
25	47	***	***		0·358
26	38	***	***	**	0·174
27	17	***	*		0·062
28	27	***	**	**	0·234
29	21	***	***		0·281
30	26	***	**		0·127
31	27	***			0·007
34	19	***	***	***	0·635
35	27	***			–0·007
37	46	***	***		0·247
38	42	***	**	*	0·149
39	39	***	*	**	0·094
40	24	***	*		0·001
41	30	***	*|		–0·003
42	29	***			–0·069
45	32	***	**|	–	0·237
46	15	***	***		0·413
47	29	***	–	*	0·413

Code	Industry	n	Coefficient (1)	Sig (1)	Coefficient (2)	Sig (2)
48 and 49	Shipbuilding and / Ship repairing	29	−0·058	***	0·145	* * ***
50	Motor vehicles	41	−0·015	**	0·396	*** *** ***
52–55	Aeroengines / Air-cushion vehicles	18	−0·064	**	0·389	* * ***
57	Engineers small tools	31	0·048	***	0·030	* ***
59	Hand tools and implements	46	0·014	***	0·140	*** *** ***
61	Yarns and threads	15	0·069	—	−0·133	— ***
63	Woollen products	25	0·113	***	−0·004	— ***
64	Hosiery	35	0·292	*** ***	0·490	** *** ***
67	Textile manufactures	41	0·096	*	0·351	* ** ***
68	Leather and fur	35	0·205	***	0·120	*** *** ***
69	Mens' tailored outerwear	30	−0·071	**	0·095	** ***
70	Womens' tailored outerwear	15	0·241	*	0·319	*** *** ***
71	Dresses, lingerie	39	0·007	*	0·234	** *** ***
72	Other clothing	43	−0·038	* *	0·073	** ** ***
73	Footwear	24	0·259	*** ***	0·291	*** *** ***
74	Bricks, fireclay	35	0·162	** **	0·349	*** *** ***
76	Glass	22	0·050	* *	0·287	** ** ***
78	Other building materials	60	−0·001	***	0·283	** ** ***
79	Furniture, bedding	41	0·144	*** ***	0·299	** *** ***
80	Timber and wood manufactures	60	0·090	** ***	0·424	** *** ***
81	Paper and board	20	0·068	*	0·281	* ***
82	Manufactures of paper	42	0·246	*** ***	0·409	*** *** ***
83	Newspapers	61	0·172	*** **	0·422	*** *** ***
84	Rubber manufactures	27	−0·028	—	0·202	** ** ***
85	Lino, leathercloth	41	0·166	***	0·070	** ** ***
86	Other manufactures	44	0·030	* **	0·180	** *** ***

Coefficient significant at: * 10% level; ** 5% level; *** 1% level.   a Negative coefficient.

Table 4. Regression results for net output minus wages and salaries.

Product group	Number of regions	Constant	X_1	X_3	X_4	X_5	$\bar{R}^2$
4 Grain milling products	43	***	***		—[a]		0·533
5 Bread, flour confectionery	49	***	***	*|			0·201
6 Bacon, meat, fish	40	—	***	*|		**	0·226
8 Cocoa, chocolate confectionery	23		**			—	0·234
9 Fruit, vegetable products	26	—	**				0·189
11 All other food products	49	**|	***			*|	0·305
12 Beer and malt	38		**	—			0·113
14 Soft drinks, cider	42	**|	***	—			0·559
23 Synthetic resins	19	—	*				0·110
25 Other chemicals	47		**		*| *		0·128
26 Iron and steel	38	**|	**		*|		0·146
27 Aluminium	17				—	—	-0·061
28 Copper, brass	27	**|	***	—	*|		0·492
29 Agricultural machinery	21		**	*	*| *	*|	0·185
30 Machine tools	26	**|					0·087
31 Pumps, valves	27	***	—		*| *		0·111
34 Construction equipment	19	—	***	*			0·337
35 Mechanical handling equipment	27	—	***	*			0·333
37 Industrial plant	46	—	***				0·282
38 Nonelectrical machinery	42	—	***				0·244
39 Other mechanical engineering	39	***	*		*| **	*|	0·250
40 Photographic equipment	24						0·093
41 Scientific instruments	30	—	**	—			0·189
42 Electrical machinery	29		**	—			0·061
45 Radio, radar	32	***	—				0·088
46 Domestic electrical goods	15					—	-0·013
47 Miscellaneous electrical goods	29	*		**		*| *	0·094

Table 5. Regression results for the efficiency index.

Product group	Number of regions	Constant	X_1	X_3	X_4	X_5	$\bar{R}^2$
4	43	***	***	—	*|	—	0·378
5	49	***		—	*| *	—	-0·010
6	40	***	***	***	—	—	0·381
8	23	***	***	**	—	—	0·440
9	26	***	***	—	**	—	0·517
11	49	***	**	—	***	—	0·124
12	38	***		*	—		0·078
14	42	***	***		—		0·585
23	19	***	***	—			0·418
25	47	***	***	—		—	0·333
26	38	***	**	**	—		0·191
27	17	***	**	**	*	**	0·290
28	27	***	***	*	—	—	0·167
29	21	***	***	**	—	**	0·361
30	26	***	**	—	*|	—	0·155
31	27	***		**	—	**	0·102
34	19	***	**	**	—		0·600
35	27	***		**	—		-0·064
37	46	***	***	—	*| *		0·311
38	42	***	***	**	—	*|	0·158
39	39	***	*	**	—	*|	0·102
40	24	***	*	—	*| *	—	0·095
41	30	***	—	—	—	—	-0·027
42	29	***	—	—		—	-0·078
45	32	***	*| *	—	—	—	0·190
46	15	***	***	—	—	—	0·207
47	29	***	—	*	—	—	0·006

Industry	n						Coefficient	Pair	n						Coefficient
48 Shipbuilding and	29	**				—	0·165	48 and 49	29	**	**		**	***	0·296
49 Ship repairing	41	**			—	—	0·011	50	41	—	**	**	***	***	0·388
50 Motor vehicles	16			—	—	—	0·216	52 –	18	*|	—	**	**	***	0·464
52 – Aeroengines	31	—		**	—	—	0·050	55	31		—	**	***	***	−0·002
55 Air-cushion vehicles	46	**		—	—	—	0·051	57	46	*|	—	**	—	***	0·140
57 Engineers small tools	15	—		—	—	*	0·129	59	15		—	—	—	***	−0·242
59 Hand tools and implements	25	—		—	—	—	0·195	61	25		—	—	—	***	−0·026
61 Yarns and threads	35	***	**	**	*	—	0·311	63	35	*	*|	***	***	***	0·521
63 Woollen products	41	***	***	*	—	***	0·183	64	41	**	***	**	***	***	0·412
64 Hosiery	35	***	***	—	***	*	0·391	67	35	*|	*|	**	**	***	0·245
67 Textile manufactures	30	**	—	—	—	—	−0·055	68	30			—	—	***	0·058
68 Leather and fur	15	—	**	**	—	—	0·253	69	15			**	***	***	0·208
69 Mens' tailored outerwear	39	**	**	***	***	—	0·238	70	39	*|		**	***	***	0·240
70 Womens' tailored outerwear	43	**	—	—	—	***	−0·017	71	43			—	—	***	0·148
71 Dresses, lingerie	24	—	**	**	*	*	0·308	72	24	*|	*	*	***	***	0·339
72 Other clothing	35	—	**	*	—	—	0·179	73	35	*|	*|	***	***	***	0·329
73 Footwear	22	***	**	—	—	—	0·205	74	22	—	—	***	*	***	0·205
74 Bricks, fireclay	60	—	—	—	—	—	0·012	76	60	—	***	***	***	***	0·434
76 Glass	41	**	—	—	—	—	0·273	78	41	**	*|	**	***	***	0·311
78 Other building materials	60	***	—	—	—	**	0·184	79	60	***	*|	**	***	***	0·434
79 Furniture, bedding	41	*	—	—	—	—	0·489	80	20	**		*	*	***	0·312
80 Timber and wood manufactures	60	***	**	—	—	***	0·321	81	42	*|	*|	*	*	***	0·392
81 Paper and board	20	—	—	—	—	***	0·190	82	61	—	—	***	***	***	0·410
82 Manufactures of paper	42	***	*	—	—	—	0·052	83	27	—	**	**	***	***	0·184
83 Newspapers	61	—	—	—	—	—	0·241	84	41			*	**	***	0·041
84 Rubber manufactures	27	—	*	—	—	**	0·061	85	41	—	—	***	***	***	0·214
85 Lino, leathercloth	41							86	44	*|	—	**	***	***	
86 Other manufactures	44														

Coefficient significant at: * 10% level; ** 5% level; *** 1% level.   a Negative coefficient.

industrially declining regions. The degree-of-urbanisation variable (X_5) has, against expectations, a negative coefficient in all but sixteen sectors, suggesting higher returns to capital in the more rural areas in the majority of sectors. This result may reflect the use of a crude variable, or the relatively recent vintage of much capital in manufacturing in the more rural areas, capital which has decentralised from the more urban areas. This movement to the 'nonmetropolitan hinterlands' has been charted in both the United States (McCarthy and Morrison, 1978) and the United Kingdom (Keeble, 1976).

The results for the same equation with Y_1 look much the same as those for Y_2. In no sectors are all four independent variables significant. The constant term is significant more frequently (in thirty-three sectors instead of seventeen), perhaps reflecting the influence of subregional differences in average wages and salaries, taken out for Y_2. The results for the efficiency index (Y_3), seen in table 5, were again better than those for Y_1 and Y_2. The constant term was again consistently significant at the 1% level and the size-of-plant variable was significant for all but twelve sectors. The size of the manufacturing labour force (X_3) was negative (and never significant) in only six sectors, being positive and significant in twenty-eight sectors. With this dependent variable, the unemployment variable has the expected negative sign for forty-three sectors, significant for fifteen of these. The degree of urbanisation is again predominantly negative, in all but fourteen sectors; being positive and significant only in shipbuilding, hosiery, and timber and wood manufactures. (This probably reflects the urban efficiency of large timber importers in ports.) The $\bar{R}^2$ values of the Y_2 equations were higher than those of the Y_1 equations in only eight sectors, while the $\bar{R}^2$ values of the Y_3 equations were higher than those of the Y_1 equations in twenty-five sectors. With none of the three dependent variables were all four independent variables both significant and of the expected sign, except hosiery for Y_3.

7 Conclusions
This paper is an early product of an attempt to establish whether agglomeration economies can be detected as having a significant influence on the productivity or efficiency of subregional aggregates of fifty-three sectors of British manufacturing industry. Special tabulations from the 1968 Census of Production allow three efficiency variables to be formed. Each has been related to the average size of plant and then to certain characteristics of each area on a cross section of up to sixty-one subregions for each sector or product group. The size of plant has been found to be an important explanatory variable for the majority of sectors; but the agglomeration variables tried so far have shown mixed success. The analysis was not possible in a further twenty-six product groups owing to insufficient observations.

Establishing the empirical importance or otherwise of the various agglomeration economies for sectors of manufacturing industry is of crucial importance to the economics of cities and regions. The implications for both theory and policy are profound and past empirical uncertainty is reflected in the divergence of views in many texts and commentaries on urban industrial expansion and regional development. Given this, an inability to establish a positive influence of the economies of agglomeration on all sectors of manufacturing industry takes on a significance in parallel to the usual statistical criteria of success in establishing association and probable causation.

Lack of success in isolating the influence of agglomeration economies in particular sectors of industry may be interpreted in several ways. Perhaps agglomeration economies really are important to a number of identifiable sectors of British manufacturing but their influence is not captured by this type of area cross-section productivity analysis. It may be that better proxy variables are needed for the sources of the economies (note, *sources* not *effects*). Possibly the data are deficient in some way (in definition, in the accuracy in collection, in aggregation, etc: perhaps the analysis should be on the basis of labour pools or city regions rather than subregions). It may be that the influence of agglomeration does not show up on the performance indicators chosen (although we may be clear that to establish the influence of agglomeration economies on growth, the more usual exercise, is different conceptually from the consideration of efficiency, as here). Perhaps the influence of agglomeration economies, though significant, is small and has not been adequately isolated from the other intraplant and intracompany factors which influence performance and may vary systematically by subregion (such as technical efficiency or the age of capital stock). It may be that the functional form of the relationships so far examined is incorrect (that is, the true form is nonadditive and/or nonlinear and/or not monotonic).

A further alternative is that the hare being chased is but a shadow in the grass: that in a spatially compact, well integrated, highly urbanised, and internationally open economy, such as that of the United Kingdom in the late 1960s, economies of agglomeration for manufacturing in many sectors are not an identifiably important influence on the productivity of either labour or capital. The importance of agglomeration for certain sectors is supported by the results offered here, even if these economies do not seem to be important for many of the engineering and metal-using sectors with which the concept of agglomeration economies has traditionally been associated. Clearly further work is required to add to and refine the variables used here and to identify more clearly the sources of agglomeration economies, where those economies exist and influence the performance of companies in particular sectors of manufacturing.

References
Aberg Y, 1973 "Regional productivity differences in Swedish manufacturing" *Regional and Urban Economies* **3**(2) 131-155
Baumol W J, 1967 "Macro-economies of unbalanced growth: the anatomy of urban crisis" *American Economic Review* **57** 415-426
Brown A J, 1972 *The Framework of Regional Economics in the United Kingdom* (Cambridge University Press, London)
Chisholm M, Oeppen J, 1973 *The Changing Pattern of Employment: Regional Specialisation and Industrial Localisation in Britain* (Croom Helm, London)
Department of Trade and Industry, 1973 "Inquiry into location attitudes and experience" memorandum submitted to the Expenditure Committee (Trade and Industry Sub-Committee) on Regional Development Incentives (Session 1973-1974, pp 525-668) HC 85-I (HMSO, London)
Economic Consultants Ltd, 1971 *Strategic Plan for the South East. Studies* volume 5 (HMSO, London)
Harris C C, Hopkins F E, 1972 *Locational Analysis: An Inter-regional Econometric Model of Agriculture, Mining, Manufacturing and Services* (Lexington Books, D C Heath, Lexington, Mass)
HMSO, 1969 *Abstract of Regional Statistics* number 5 (HMSO, London)
HMSO, 1973 *Input Output Tables for 1968* (HMSO, London)
HMSO, 1974 *Report on the Census of Production 1968. Volume 157. Summary Tables: Area Analyses* (HMSO, London)
Keeble D E, 1969 "Local industrial linkage and manufacturing growth in outer London" *Town Planning Review* **40**(2) 163-188
Keeble D E, 1976 *Industrial Location and Planning in Britain* (Methuen, London)
Keeble D E, Hauser D P, 1971 "Spatial analysis of manufacturing growth in outer south east England 1960-1967, I. Hypotheses and variables" *Regional Studies* **5** 229-262
Keeble D E, Hauser D P, 1972 "Spatial analysis of manufacturing growth in outer south east England 1960-1967, II. Methods and results" *Regional Studies* **6** 11-36
Laos E H, 1977 *The Sources of Regional Differences in Efficiency. The Case of Mexican Manufacturing* PhD thesis, University of East Anglia, Norwich
Lever W F, 1972 "Industrial movement, spatial association and functional linkages" *Regional Studies* **6**(4) 371-384
Lever W F, 1974 "Manufacturing linkages and the search for supplies and markets" in *Spatial Perspectives on Industrial Organisation and Decision Making* Ed. F E I Hamilton (John Wiley, Chichester, Sussex)
McCarthy K F, Morrison P A, 1978 "The changing demographic and economic structure of non metropolitan areas in the 1970s" *International Regional Science Review* **2**(2) 123-142
Mitchell B, 1978 "Measuring value added from the Census of Production" *Statistical News* **41** 4-9
Moseley M J, Townroe P M, 1973 "Linkage adjustment following industrial movement" *Tijdschrift voor Economische en Sociale Geografie* **64**(3) 137-144
Richardson H W, 1973 *Regional Growth Theory* (Macmillan, London)
Richardson H W, 1974 "Empirical aspects of regional growth in the United States" *Annals of Regional Science* **8**(2) 8-23
Richter C E, 1969 "The impact of industrial linkages on geographic association" *Journal of Regional Science* **9**(1) 19-28
Sant M E C, 1975 *Industrial Movement and Regional Development: The British Case* (Pergamon Press, Oxford)
Streit M E, 1969 "Spatial associations and economic linkages between industries" *Journal of Regional Science* **9**(2) 177-189
Wheat L F, 1973 *Regional Economic Growth and Industrial Location* (D C Heath, Lexington, Mass)

APPENDIX

The index of efficiency
In simplified notation

$$\pi_i = \frac{Q_i}{Q} \Big/ \left(\alpha \frac{L_i}{L} + \beta \frac{K_i}{K} \right) , \tag{A1}$$

where Q_i, L_i, and K_i are the values of net output and the labour and capital input of the industry in subregion i, and Q, L, and K are the values for the industry nationally and are the national shares of labour and capital in income.

If equation (A1) is divided by (L_i/L) we obtain

$$\pi_i = \frac{q_i}{q} \Big/ \left(\alpha + \beta \frac{k_i}{k} \right) , \tag{A2}$$

where

$$q_i = \frac{Q_i}{L_i} , \qquad q = \frac{Q}{L} , \qquad k_i = \frac{K_i}{L_i} , \qquad k = \frac{K}{L} .$$

Information is available on q_i, q, α_i, and α.

If W_i is the wage bill for the industry in subregion i and r_i is the cost of capital, then labour's share in the subregion,

$$\alpha_i = \frac{W_i}{Q_i} = 1 - r_i \frac{K_i}{Q_i} = 1 - \frac{r_i K_i}{q_i L_i} .$$

Now

$$k_i = \frac{K_i}{L_i} = (1 - \alpha_i) \frac{q_i}{r_i}$$

and

$$k = \frac{K}{L} = (1 - \alpha) \frac{q}{r} ,$$

so

$$\frac{k_i}{k} = \frac{(1 - \alpha_i) q_i}{(1 - \alpha) q}$$

if we assume that $r_i = r_j = r$. Now substituting into equation (A2) with $\beta = 1 - \alpha$,

$$\pi_i = \frac{q_i}{q} \Big/ \left[\alpha + (1 - \alpha_i) \frac{q_i}{q} \right] = 1 \Big/ \left(\alpha \frac{q}{q_i} + 1 - \alpha_i \right) .$$

The Standard Metropolitan Labour Area Concept Revisited

M G COOMBES, J S DIXON, J B GODDARD, S OPENSHAW, P J TAYLOR
University of Newcastle upon Tyne

1 Introduction

In recent years there has been a growing interest in the identification of functional regions centred on urban areas. In particular, such regions have been used for intranational, and latterly international, studies of population and economic data (Hall et al, 1973; Smart, 1974; Drewett et al, 1976; Hay and Hall, 1976) following earlier work to produce standard metropolitan statistical areas (SMSAs) for the USA Census (US Bureau of the Census, 1951). This interest in functional regionalisation largely reflects a concern that current political and administrative boundaries no longer provide a meaningful definition of the functional organisation of urban areas. However, the units that such boundaries define are not comparable. Thus the statement that Liverpool has less population than Manchester is quite meaningless since it is unclear what is meant by Liverpool and Manchester. Presumably we do not wish to restrict these entities to their respective metropolitan district or county borough boundaries thereby missing out the important areas of Bootle and Salford respectively. This is both a basic geographical problem concerning the definition of meaningful urban systems and a manifestation of the modifiable areal unit problem. This problem arises whenever data have been aggregated to an arbitrary spatial framework (Openshaw, 1977), resulting in changes to the distribution of values in the original information on individuals. The solution is therefore to provide a meaningful and useful reporting frame, such as a set of functional urban areas, for national census data.

This paper presents the results of a series of attempts to replicate one of the major functional regionalisations of Britain: that produced by researchers at the London School of Economics (LSE) (Drewett et al, 1974). Previous researchers have shown a far greater propensity to spawn new regionalisations than to examine the nature and properties of previous definitions. Furthermore, it is apparent that before very long a decision will be made concerning precisely which, if any, of the alternative regionalisations to accept as a framework for presenting statistics for cities in the 1981 Census of Britain. The importance of this is accentuated by the four-fold reduction in the number of local authority units following the 1974 reorganisation of local government. As base areas for Census data, these new units provide a poorer framework for analytical purposes than the previous areas, which at least had the virtue of being historically based on physical urban areas and their local rural hinterlands (originating in 19th-century Poor Law and sanitary legislation). If a specially designed areal framework is actually going to be used for reporting 1981 Census results, then it is particularly important to ensure that it is not as arbitrary as the frameworks it is meant to replace and that its properties are known and understood. An independent reexamination of the consistency and meaningfulness of the set of functional urban areas most widely used at present, the LSE standard metropolitan labour areas (SMLAs), is thus imperative.

Section 2 of this paper outlines the nature of the SMLA approach which is to be replicated and the computer algorithm used to implement it. Section 3 describes the results of attempting to replicate the SMLAs of Drewett et al (1976) and of the search for empirical evidence to support the decision rules that they adopted. Section 4 reports the findings of additional experiments with the SMLA-type of definition and discusses some of the more general points raised by the attempted replication. It also describes the emergence of an alternative regionalisation with an arguably better empirical and conceptual basis, and discusses its utility as a framework for reporting 1981 census results.

2 Identifying SMLAs
2.1 The case for replication
The replication of the SMLA regions was undertaken for the constructive purpose of checking their suitability as functional urban areas for the 1981 Census. This exercise follows that of Berry et al (1968) which found a bewildering variety of alternatives for the definition of US SMSAs and much dissatisfaction with present definitional practice. In this paper the claim by Drewett et al (1976, page 2) that the SMLAs are the product of a "definition of a set of functional urban areas using criteria consistently", is put to the test as were the similar claims by the US Bureau of the Census. Furthermore, research has shown that spatial classifications of Census data are sensitive to apparently minor operational decisions during the application of statistical techniques (Openshaw and Gillard, 1979). This research constitutes excellent a priori grounds for suspecting similar, or even worse, problems in the identification of SMLAs.

Another reason for wanting to replicate the SMLA definitions was the extensive use of manual rather than computer techniques by the LSE team. It is thought likely that the restrictions of this manual process may have resulted in errors of application. It also allows the possibility for the rules to be bent in order to accommodate special cases known to the researchers. In fact Drewett et al (1976) provide no details of the problems they must have faced. However, a good example of this type of difficulty is given in Hay and Hall when they report "... eight single cores do not meet criterion (b) ... but are included ..." (Hay and Hall, 1976, page 4). Of course, there are always good reasons to justify 'rule bending' but if this occurs then strictly speaking it should be reported and the results can no longer claim to have been produced by the consistent application of fixed criteria. Moreover, there is always a danger that other cases which are equally good candidates for rule bending do not come to the attention of the researchers.

Another characteristic feature of these previous attempts to define functional urban areas is their addiction to a very crude form of taxonomy. Basically a series of arbitrary rules are produced and applied (see section 2.2). Their justification is largely in conceptual terms and there has been a notable absence of any empirical analysis to support the rules which are adopted. This omission is very serious indeed when the entire basis for the SMLA type of definition is a set of arbitrary rules, most of which were in any case imported unchanged from the US Census (see for example the comparison given in Drewett et al, 1976, appendix note 1). There has been virtually no opportunity for the data to 'speak for themselves' in the selection of definitional criteria. Perhaps minor adjustments to the inherited thresholds would find natural breaks in the data. The replication exercise below will consider these issues for the most-used set of functional urban areas, the LSE SMLAs. Moreover, it is also a useful preliminary stage in investigating the usefulness of the SMLA concept in the broader context of searching for a better basis for a set of national functional urban areas.

2.2 The overall approach

The definitions used in the Drewett et al (1976) identification of SMLAs are based on Hall et al (1973), but applied to 1971 Census data. These in turn originated from US Census definitions with only minor modifications for the British situation. Thus the principles of SMLA definition are rooted in those of the US Bureau of the Budget (1964, page 1), which aim "to identify an integrated economic and social unit with a recognised large population nucleus". This concept is in practice interpreted as a nodal region, so that the first step is to isolate the urban centres. This version of an integrated region is completed by defining the hinterlands of these urban centres. Data on the interaction of the small areas used in these definitions is scarce so the criteria for the integration of centres and hinterlands are restricted to journey-to-work flows. To be consistent with this bias towards employment distribution, British studies (Hall et al, 1973; Drewett et al, 1974) have used employment rather than population as the measure of minimum size for the urban centre. In defence of this step, it has been extensively argued (for example Coombes et al, 1978) that daily urban systems (such as SMLAs) which are defined by using journey-to-work data form a good approximation to general-purpose functional regions. This nodal-region approach is manifest in the LSE definitions (Drewett et al, 1974).

The basic SMLA algorithm consisted of the following steps:
Step 1. From the set of pre-1974 local authority (LA) building blocks identify as urban cores those units with *either* an employment density of five workers per acre *or* a total employment of at least 20000 jobs.

Step 2. Consider amalgamation of cores which are contiguous.

Step 3. Allocate to each core, all those unallocated LAs which have more than 15% of their workers commuting to it, and are contiguous to the core or to another LA already allocated to it. These form what is termed the Inner Metropolitan Ring.

Step 4. The result of steps 1, 2, and 3 are termed standard metropolitan labour areas (SMLAs) and would normally have a minimum population of 70000. SMLAs with less than this minimum would be deleted, and the constituent units considered for reallocation to other SMLAs.

Step 5. The remaining unallocated LAs are assigned to whatever core they send the highest proportion of their working residents to, provided they are contiguous to one or more of its members. This forms what is termed the outer metropolitan ring. The results of steps 1–5 is termed the metropolitan economic labour area (MELA).

It should also be noted that it is possible to have a SMLA consisting of a core without a ring and a MELA without an outer ring; for example, where several employment nodes occur in close proximity. The results of applying this procedure to 1732 LAs resulted in 126 urban cores, seven of which have no metropolitan rings and thirty-three no outer rings. In 1971 79·3% of the population lived in the SMLAs, and 95·7% in the MELAs (Drewett et al, 1976, page 4). For the present paper, attention will generally be limited to SMLAs, since the outer rings of MELAs are far more sensitive to the different cutoffs used for published journey-to-work data in the Census volumes (which were the data source for the LSE study) and the computer-readable tapes available to the authors.

2.3 The basic computer algorithm
At first sight the process of defining SMLAs, as outlined above, seems so simple that it is somewhat surprising that it has not been previously computerised. In fact this is largely a result not of the complexity of the classification procedure but an absence of data in computer-readable form. Thus, where the data were initially available only in printed form, there was not much incentive for computer processes. This study is unusual in that it was conceived as a computer application with all data on magnetic tapes. This entailed the numerical interpretation of the contiguity constraint in the SMLA definition, a problem avoided by the manual procedure of earlier studies.

For present purposes a set of subroutines have been written which not only provide an SMLA program, but also allow for various modifications to the criteria and for changes in the sequence of the rules. When these subroutines are structured to conform with the SMLA algorithm previously described, the result is a program with approximately 2500 FORTRAN source statements. A run to identify cores, SMLAs, and MELAs typically requires 384K bytes of memory and seven seconds of CPU time on an IBM 370/168.

It is suggested that computerisation is needed to ensure absolute consistency in the application of rules, to permit a fuller examination of instances where a manual procedure would be restricted to a small number of possible permutations of building blocks, and to enable the effects of changes in the criteria to be identified quickly. In the event, the most difficult part of the entire process is getting the computer to decide intelligently in an automatic manner which is the most meaningful name to allocate to each of the regions that are produced!

2.4 The data
The data used for this analysis are essentially copies of that used by Drewett et al (1976) but with a few additions. It was decided to make use of data for split LAs which the Office of Population Censuses and Surveys produced in a vain attempt to anticipate local government reorganisation. Additionally, it was necessary to use New Town areas, since the use of whole LA areas in the LSE study effectively excluded all but Phase 1 New Towns. The result was a set of about 1850 building blocks for which the standard Census population and household data are available. In addition each area is located by means of a National Grid coordinate and measured in hectares. Finally, a contiguity matrix was compiled and coded for the computer, together with a comprehensive classification of different contiguity types.

The major data-processing problem was the need to store the journey-to-work data in an efficient manner; a file with potentially sixteen million characters of information in it. In practice this problem was greatly simplified by the use of sparse matrix techniques, methods which were also used for storing the contiguity matrix. Nevertheless it is readily apparent that the size of the problem would preclude the straightforward application of several alternative methods of functional regionalisation which may have seemed appropriate. For example the network procedure of Slater (1976), the transaction-flow algorithm of Leusmann and Slater (1977), and the intramax algorithm of Masser and Brown (1975) have all been developed for use with interaction matrices far smaller than the 1930 zone matrix used here.

3 Replicating the LSE SMLAs
3.1 An investigation of consistency
This paper is not in fact concerned with evaluating the data produced by alternative functional regionalisations of Britain, but with exploring the classificatory mechanisms themselves. In some ways this is less useful

than the former, but it is argued that it is absolutely basic and must precede any subsequent and more rigorous evaluations. Attention is thus restricted to the consistency in which the rules are applied and the meaningfulness of the rules themselves in relation to the data. Brief mention has already been made of the background of the SMLA type of regionalisation. Another paper by the authors (Coombes et al, 1978) has been cited concerning the general relevance of regions defined by employment and journey-to-work data. Rather than expand this theoretical justification of the approach of which SMLAs are an example, this paper first turns to the problems of a consistent application of this approach. The question to be answered is whether such an application is possible which translates the apparent theoretical reasonableness of the SMLA concept into geographically sensible regions.

3.2 Literal replication

Tables 1 and 2 compare the results, in the upper and lower size ranges respectively, of the LSE work of Drewett et al (1976) and various SMLA-type regionalisations by the authors. The LSE definitions ('SMLA 1') produce 126 SMLAs in all, as stated on table 3. In terms of the more numerous base units of the current study, this regionalisation assigned 239 units to cores and 696 to rings (plus 553 in the MELA outer rings and 442 unassigned). The current study initially attempted to replicate these figures, originally as a focus for the development of the computerized SMLA algorithm. An indication of alternative sets of rules, and their effects on the regions produced, could be derived from a brief analysis of the sensitivity of the SMLA algorithm's specification (section 2.2).

The least well-defined component in the SMLA definition is the notion of contiguity. This deceptively simple concept proves imprecise to operationalise (Coombes, 1978). The principal reason is that it is required simultaneously to represent quite different factors, such as the sharing of a boundary by administrative areas, close physical proximity, or substantial interaction between a pair of areas. For example, unless offshore islands are to be excluded from any regionalisation, the contiguity constraint must recognise their links with mainland areas with which they share no boundary. However, the amalgamation of core units in step 2 would then create, for example, a single region centred jointly upon Aberdeen and Kirkwall (in the Orkneys) unless this nonboundary link between the two is identified as such and then ignored in the automated amalgamation subroutine. This interpretation was adopted at the outset in the computerised replication of the LSE algorithm (SMLA 2). In the algorithm specification (section 2.2) step 4 follows Hall et al (1973) and Drewett et al (1974) in asserting that the SMLA population threshold is 70 000. However, despite a considerable 'natural break' below 75 000, the effective threshold used was 60 000 (note the entries for SMLA 1 below 70 000 in table 2). SMLA 3 therefore follows Hay and Hall (1976) in adopting the

Table 1. Ranking of largest SMLAs by population by different regionalisations.

Rank	SMLA 1	SMLA 2/SMLA 3	SMLA 4/SMLA 5	SMLA 6
1	London	London	London	London
2	Birmingham	Birmingham	Birmingham	Birmingham
3	Manchester	Manchester	Manchester	Manchester
4	Glasgow	Liverpool	Glasgow	Glasgow
5	Liverpool	Leicester	Liverpool	Liverpool
6	Leeds	Glasgow	Leeds	Newcastle
7	Newcastle	Leeds	Newcastle	Leeds
8	Sheffield	Newcastle	Sheffield	Sheffield
9	Coventry	Sheffield	Bristol	Bristol
10	Bristol	Bristol	Edinburgh	Edinburgh
11	Edinburgh	Edinburgh	Nottingham	Nottingham
12	Nottingham	Teesside	Teesside	Leicester
13	Leicester	Portsmouth	Leicester	Stoke
14	Stoke	Stoke	Portsmouth	Cardiff
15	Portsmouth	Southampton	Stoke	Southampton
16	Teesside	Cardiff	Southampton	Coventry

Table 2. Ranking of SMLAs with under 70000 population by different regionalisations.

SMLA 1	SMLA 2	SMLA 3	SMLA 4	SMLA 5
Crawley	none	Crawley	Crawley	Crawley
Yeovil		Stevenage	Stevenage	Stevenage
Perth		Ashford	Loughborough	Loughborough
Ashford		Scarborough	Maidenhead	Maidenhead
Salisbury		Bracknell	Ashford	Ashford
Ellesmere Port		East Kilbride	Scarborough	Scarborough
		Perth	East Kilbride	East Kilbride
		Merthyr Tydfil	Perth	Perth
		Leyland	Merthyr Tydfil	Merthyr Tydfil
		Corby	Leyland	
			Corby	

Table 3. Assignment of base units by different regionalisations.

	Number of SMLAs/MELAs	Base units			
		cores	inner rings	outer rings	excluded
SMLA 1	126	239	696	553	442
SMLA 2	117	292	674	586	378
SMLA 3	127	311	675	590	354
SMLA 4	135	295	654	612	359
SMLA 5	128	283	660	617	370
SMLA 6	83	180	525	718	507
SMLA 7	82	325	699	557	349
SMLA 8	147	313	689	617	311

Table 1 (continued)

Rank	SMLA 7	SMLA 8
1	London	London
2	Birmingham	Birmingham
3	Manchester	Manchester
4	Liverpool	Glasgow
5	Leeds	Liverpool
6	Glasgow	Leeds
7	Newcastle	Newcastle
8	Southampton	Sheffield
9	Sheffield	Bristol
10	Bristol	Edinburgh
11	Swansea	Nottingham
12	Edinburgh	Teesside
13	Teesside	Leicester
14	Stoke	Portsmouth
15	Cardiff	Stoke
16	Hull	Southampton

Table 2 continued

SMLA 6	SMLA 7	SMLA 8	
Crawley	Ashford	Crawley	Pontypridd
Stevenage	Scarborough	Folkestone	Salisbury
East Kilbride	Perth	Stevenage	Banbury
Leyland		Loughborough	Leyland
		Maidenhead	Corby
		Ashford	Dumfries
		Scarborough	
		Bracknell	plus thirteen more with
		East Kilbride	50000–60000
		Perth	population
		Accrington	

lower standard. This increases the number of our base units assigned to cores from 292 to 311, and increases the number of rings from 674 to 675 (table 3). The 60000 threshold was incorporated, with the refinement in the contiguity constraint above, as a change to the standard algorithm.

Superficially the difference of only one region between the LSE total (SMLA 1) and that of the SMLA 3 replication is impressive. However, it disguises very considerable variations in the actual results, not least the gain of several SMLAs based on New Towns, as shown by table 2. The balancing losses are less easy to categorise, but many are at least partially the result of the rigorous automated contiguity constraint. Most notable is the loss of Nottingham from the entry for SMLA 2/3 in table 1 (the change to the minimum population not affecting these largest SMLAs, hence the common entry in table 1). Nottingham disappears owing to a string of large rural districts which link up the whole of the East Midlands to create a single SMLA. Although nominally centred on Leicester, its core is an uninterrupted chain of base units all exceeding the 20 000 jobs threshold of step 1. It would seem therefore that there was an unstated assumption by earlier researchers that only areas with urban status in a legal sense (for example, county boroughs and not rural districts) were to be considered for core status. SMLA 4 implements this unstated condition; table 3 showing that eight more regions result, with sixteen fewer base units in cores. This alteration was added to the standard algorithm (section 2.2).

A less dramatic difference between SMLA 1 and SMLA 3/4 is instanced by the emergence of a Leyland SMLA (table 2). This town satisfies the employment-density criterion of step 1 and, with its rings, passes the regional-population minimum. In general, areas passing the density but not the absolute employment criterion do not survive as cores (because their small size leads to a region which is below the population threshold) unless they become amalgamated with larger core areas. Hall et al (1973) introduced the density criterion especially to consolidate the major core areas, but omitted to specify that every region should possess at least one core unit which passes the absolute employment criterion. Table 3 shows that the result of the inclusion of this unstated constraint to SMLA 5 is the loss of only seven SMLAs compared with the results for SMLA 4, but to those interested in those particular areas (for example, Leyland) this amount of change is not trivial but fundamental.

The majority of the critical issues in SMLA regionalisation concern the first steps in the algorithm. This is because the number of base areas that are identified as cores, and their distribution and amalgamation, overwhelmingly influence the final results. This has been clearly shown by the effects of the reinterpretation of the SMLA algorithm, and even the implementation of previously unspecified constraints (legal urban status for every core unit and at least one unit passing the absolute employment threshold in each amalgamated core). By the inclusion of each of these developments, the subsequent run of the algorithm produced results which approached more closely a replication of the original (SMLA 1) regionalisation, but without achieving that aim.

3.3 Replicating the spirit rather than the letter

The automation of the SMLA algorithm has caused problems for the replication exercise by the literal and consistent application of a set of criteria which were intended to be applied with discretion. The question arises as to whether or not it is possible to match the spirit of the SMLA approach by modifying the stated decision rules and thereby attempt to move closer to the results that were produced by Drewett et al (1974), the SMLA 1 regionalisation which was produced by hand.

A crucial difference of treatment which has not been replicated is that of London. Earlier studies assume that only the inner areas were within the core of the London SMLA, although all London boroughs clearly pass the 20000 jobs criterion. This is the result of the sheer size of these base units. Those Outer London boroughs excluded from the LSE London core can be discriminated by raising the employment-density threshold from 12·355 jobs per hectare (five per acre) to 13·3. However, exclusion of these units, which still satisfy the total-employment conditions, requires that the criterion be changed from satisfaction of either of these thresholds to satisfaction of them both. SMLA 6 therefore alters step 1 of the algorithm from 'OR' to 'AND' whilst slightly raising the density threshold. Table 3 shows that this reduces qualifying core units by over one hundred, while table 1 emphasises that this replication attempt has resulted in the loss of the SMLA centred on the overbounded Teesside county borough. Clearly this modification moves the results further from those of SMLA 1. Consequently this adjustment to the SMLA algorithm is rejected, with the London problem unsolved.

The major remaining obstacle to replication derives from the apparently selective suspension of the contiguity constraint on the amalgamation of core units by the manual SMLA 1 regionalisation. Thus there are a number of regions with polynuclear cores. For example, neither Workington nor Whitehaven passes either density or absolute-employment criteria although together they muster over 20000 jobs and are designated a joint core. On the other hand, Rugby, Leamington, and Nuneaton all surpass this threshold but were subsumed into Coventry's core. However, in none of these cases are these units contiguous, although there may be only one intervening area. An attempt was consequently made (SMLA 7) to build such regions consistently by allowing the amalgamation of cores which were not directly contiguous, but were both contiguous to a 'third party' area. Unfortunately this reduced the total number of SMLAs to only eighty-two, although the number of base units in the cores is higher than for any other regionalisation in table 3. For example, the successful replication of the Coventry amalgam is supplemented by its amalgamation with Birmingham and the Black Country and (also a single rural district away) the East Midland complex through Leicester to Nottingham. The new amalgamation routine of SMLA 7 reconstitutes this grouping (dismantled earlier by the urban status requirement) within a single huge SMLA covering the Midlands. Again this fails to replicate SMLA 1, while leaving untouched the other problem, those cores which are contiguous but were still not amalgamated in SMLA 1 (for example, Guildford and Woking). There seems no way of adapting the existing SMLA algorithm to accommodate these exceptions in a procedure that is automated and thus globally consistent.

3.4 Data exploration in search of evidence

The inability to replicate the LSE SMLAs has been accompanied by the failure to identify a version of the SMLA algorithm which generates intuitively meaningful results. The next step seems to be a look at the data to see whether or not criteria can be identified which may result in a 'natural' SMLA type of classification. Perhaps this may also indicate a regionalisation which would produce results without intuitively obvious failings.

The local-authority data base was therefore investigated to evaluate the influence upon classifications of the base units of their original definition as either urban or rural units. For example, would there tend to be bimodal distributions caused by these areas being either tightly bounded urban districts or relatively extensive rural districts? In fact, gross inconsistencies in the definition of these pre-1974 administrative units results in a continuum of values for all the variables. Figure 1 illustrates this distribution for the variable, total employment.

Figure 2 plots the two SMLA core criteria variables, total employment and employment density. Both axes have been bisected at the standard SMLA thresholds. The original step 1 criterion approves as cores all units passing either density or absolute threshold. Thus all entries on the plot except those in the lower-left part are cores. A different approach would be to require the satisfaction of *both* thresholds (whether at these or different levels) and therefore to accept as cores only those base units falling in the upper-right quarter.

The very limited results of the search for natural thresholds among the primary data indicates the need for a further step; a thorough sensitivity testing of the SMLA algorithm. For example, figure 3 confirms the

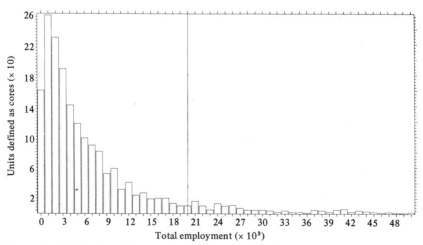

Figure 1. Distribution of base unit values for total employment.

futility of the search for a natural threshold for the core criterion of total employment: the number of cores found rises smoothly with the lowering of the threshold. Moreover the secondary criterion of density (three widely differing values having been coupled with each step along the employment axis) has little effect on this regular result of the numbers of cores found.

Finally, figure 4 shows the result of completing the regionalisation algorithm for each of these combinations of employment criteria. Although the density variable again has little influence, the number of regions now fluctuates interestingly with the change of the absolute criterion. Because figure 3 showed that lowering the total-employment

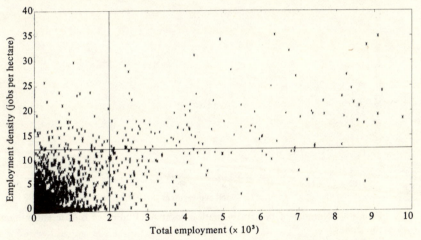

Figure 2. Distribution of base unit values for employment and employment density.

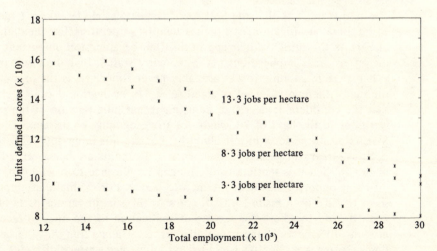

Figure 3. Number of base units in cores with different employment and density thresholds.

threshold brings a steady increase in the number of cores, this suggests
that the locational characteristics of these marginal cores are significantly
clustered along this axis. At some points along this axis the number of
SMLAs actually falls with the introduction of more cores, demonstrating
that at those particular employment size ranges there are groups of base
units which tend to be bridging gaps between separate cores. Thus when
the threshold is lowered the intervening unit becomes a core and so creates
a single contiguous core where there had previously been two.

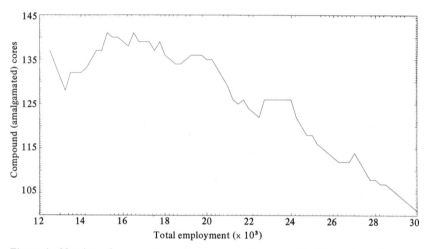

Figure 4. Number of postamalgamation compound cores with different employment
thresholds.

3.5 Some general comments

The results indicate that the SMLAs of Drewett et al (1976) are largely
an intuitive classification. In their attempt to operationalise the definition
of SMLAs the spirit of their approach often became more important than
the letter. It is implicit, but never explicitly stated, that the result is not
a 'hard' classification. It was probably never conceived as the product of
the rigid adherence to a set of fixed rules. In mitigation it can be claimed
that the considerable degree of adjustment and modification of the results
was done in the light of knowledge of the geography of Britain. Thus the
SMLAs produced look intuitively right, but are not internally consistent.

However, it can be argued that when assignments are being carried out
manually then it is sensible to use human intelligence to react to the
different opportunities with the map to hand. For example, attempts
seem to have been made to 'find' cores to fill gaps in various parts of the
country, and to adjust the manner of application of the rules to take into
account differences in the base units. It is certainly true that the building
blocks differ from Scotland to England. Inverness-shire is different from
Essex, hence the problems with using fixed rules. For example, the use

of an 'AND' criterion in the first step of the algorithm of SMLA 6 yielded unacceptable results when applied to the whole data set, although it replicated the intuitively reasonable treatment of London by SMLA 1.

This is not a simple problem, and perhaps is inevitable when a large-scale exercise is carried out by manual means within a tight research schedule. There is little doubt that the SMLAs as identified represented a compromise between a set of rules, intuitive expectations of what the results should be, and a manual methodology. There may be nothing wrong with this sort of compromise, but it is misleading to fail to detail these perambulations and claim that the results have all the properties they would have had if a systematic and consistently applied procedure had been used. The general methodological issue that arises from these considerations is the need for the limitations of any system of classification to be fully explored. It may be necessary to accept that some existing intuitively reasonable regionalisations are inconsistent or inappropriate when subject to empirical investigation and replication.

From this, the question arises as to whether or not it makes sense to demand that SMLAs be consistently defined according to a fixed set of global criteria. It is suggested that the answer must be yes if the aim is to produce a framework for national studies of Census data. In a definitional situation it is necessary to be explicit and also intersubjective; otherwise the result is woolly research. Consequently our analysis continues to reexamine the data base in all its variations, seeking a definition of the SMLA concept which is sufficiently flexible in its rules to produce sensible results when applied consistently across the country.

4 Searching for an alternative
4.1 A modified SMLA approach
The work of replicating the SMLA definitions has thrown up numerous possible improvements to the established algorithm. Already mentioned a number of times above, the first such modification is the replacement in step 1 of an 'AND' criterion for the 'OR' (that is, cores would be restricted to units satisfying *both* employment-total *and* employment-density thresholds). This would need to be coupled with a lowering of the employment-density threshold, as numerous overbounded large centres such as Teesside and Sheffield fall well below five jobs per acre. Experiments have concentrated upon combining these changes with a reduction of the total-employment threshold to around 15 000. This seems to be a level around which results are more stable in the sensitivity tests above (figure 4) than the 20 000 mark used elsewhere. This alteration is carried forward into a phase of experiment on the SMLA criteria.

Numerous instances above have shown the sensitivity of all SMLA results to the contiguity constraint which causes the amalgamation of core units and so individuates the potential regions. A measure of the interdependence of cores (through journey-to-work flows) can be used in addition or instead of the simple contiguity of sometimes meaningless legal areas. Little radical change can be expected of such a modification because in the vast majority of cases a contiguity link between areas is a good indication of close proximity which (owing to distance deterrence effects) usually implies a reasonable level of interaction. Of course, the analysis above has shown that the few exceptions to this generalisation are sufficient to make a classification unacceptable, so that efforts to devise a more sophisticated and relevant amalgamation routine are necessary. The introduction of an interaction constraint on core amalgamation would provide a further threshold which could be experimented with to assess the effects on the results. The changes may be few numerically but they can be critical geographically, and changes from the results of SMLA 1 are inevitable with the consistent application of any algorithm.

4.2 A new framework

It has now become apparent that a natural classification of functional urban areas is not easily going to drop out of the data. Some order seemed to exist but the available classificatory techniques, based on a priori definitional rules, seemed incapable of or inadequate for the task. One possible explanation is that so far only univariate criteria have been applied to a multivariate problem. Yet the advantages of simplicity associated with this approach are seen as an important factor in any subsequent attempts to persuade government agencies to use functional urban areas as reporting units for the 1981 Census.

The first part of the solution is to develop a clearer conceptual notion of what the end product should be, and then use this as a basis for identifying the rules for producing it. In a previous paper (Coombes et al, 1978) the authors attempted to justify use of the concept of daily urban systems (DUSs) to define meaningful areal units for reporting the 1981 Census. A theoretical argument was presented in favour of functional urban areas as opposed to the traditional administrative, political, or euclidean (grid square) units. These arguments, of course, provide a justification for the previously discussed SMLAs, which are also examples of DUSs. At this point, then, it is necessary to describe the sort of spatial structure that the authors prefer as an alternative to previous British DUS regionalisations.

First of all, it is suggested that the resulting classification should have discrete zones, so that an area sending commuters to two cities can only be allocated to the DUS of one city. This is a pragmatic requirement for ease of presentation of results, although in reality the total DUSs for adjacent cities will frequently overlap. The DUS approach in practice produces urban systems centered on a single city or compact group of urban areas.

This basic constraint imposes a simple structure on the regionalisation which works well in rural areas with large market towns, but is far less appropriate in older industrial areas. Previous British applications of the DUS concept have always produced a single-tier regionalisation, so that the urban hierarchy which underlies the distribution of cities has not been employed as part of the system of classification. Thus previous regionalisations have defined DUSs centred on, for instance Liverpool and Taunton, with no account taken of the vast difference in nature between these two areas. A single-tier classification has the basic advantage of simplicity but it implies comparability between areal units that most researchers would consider to be unlike. This is a problem which presents difficulties to any regionalisation which does not take into account the differences between the more and the less urbanized parts of Britain.

Finally, there is the problem of whether the classification should exhaust the national territory. Clearly not all parts of Britain fall into DUSs around the recognised urban centres, indeed a 'nonmetropolitan' residual is typical of previous regionalisations. Hay and Hall (1976) divide the peripheral areas into nonurban regions using nonnodal criteria derived from Smart (1974). However, the use of two distinct classification procedures undermines the basic advantage of exhausting the national territory by allocating all areas to urban-centred regions in a single complete classification: the requirement of consistency has been broached.

It is unlikely that any single urban-region framework will perfectly resolve these issues. The aim must be the most careful mix of concepts which together will ensure that the classification will have the general-purpose relevance vital for the presentation of Census data. This requirement includes both the statistical suitability of the areas for data aggregation and their intuitive acceptability as geographic entities.

4.3 A two-tier functional regionalisation

The failure to replicate the LSE SMLA regionalisation, or to find a natural DUS classification, has led to an analysis of the problems in functional regionalisation. The inadequacy of a single-tier structure of nonoverlapping DUSs leads to the suggestion of a system of free-standing DUSs plus metropolitan city regions. The latter would be composed of complexes of DUSs and be found in the highly urbanised areas. In these units there would be a second tier, each region having a central, *dominant* DUS plus other DUSs which are *subdominant* to it, to use the terminology of Bogue (1949). This idea recognises the relationship between, for instance, Liverpool and Southport, whereas in previous classifications these are separate DUSs despite large absolute commuter flows from the smaller centre to the larger centre and hinterland. The new approach allows Southport to be recognised as a local subdominant centre within the metropolitan region based on Liverpool. In contrast, the free-standing DUSs are based on cities or towns which qualify as separate 'cores', but which neither dominate other DUSs nor are themselves dominated.

It has been found that the use of a measure of self-containment (the proportion of an area's residents who work locally) provides a sound basis for the measurement of the subdominance of a DUS. This calculation highlights the extent of the commuting from a smaller, peripheral DUS to a metropolitan centre. Owing to the 50 000 (or more) minimum population of DUSs, a self-containment measure of less than 95% represents an extensive degree of out-commuting. These subdominant DUSs can then be associated with the dominant DUSs with which they have their major residual (extra-DUS) commuting flows. Those DUSs which are neither subdominant nor the dominant centres of metropolitan regions, become free-standing: they remain separate DUSs at the upper tier of city regions (a good example might be Carlisle).

Thus the two-tier approach presents a flexible but consistent DUS regionalisation. It recognizes the metropolitan hierarchy without the ad hoc and arbitrary rulings adopted in the USA to create standard consolidated statistical areas from the individual SMSAs. The two-tier structure represents the simplest way of overcoming the problem of the differences between the more urbanised regions and the peripheral areas. Clearly a hierarchy limited to one or two tiers remains a simplification, but further elaboration would seem likely to result in an unacceptable loss of clarity. The second tier is sufficient to illustrate the wholely different structure of the rural areas, whose large market towns form a network of free-standing DUSs, without subdominant satellite urban areas like those around the principal metropolitan cities.

On the other hand, the more complex patterns of activity in the major urbanised regions are reflected in the derivation of a second tier in the regionalisation. Two types of commuting flow, local and longer distance, are accommodated within the metropolitan structure. Although the majority of work trips are internalised within DUS boundaries, significant flows occur from the satellite DUSs to the dominant DUS. This pattern emphasises the differences in the mobility of socioeconomic groups, 'white-collar' workers usually forming the majority of long-distance commuters. This section of the community is also likely to make more frequent trips from the outlying DUSs (such as Southport) to the metropolitan centres (such as Liverpool) for the higher-order shopping, recreation, and other functions provided there for the whole metropolitan city region.

SMLA 8 (tables 1–3) provides an example of a set of DUSs which would be suitable as a lower tier of the kind of regionalisation defined above. The number of core units has been increased by the lowering of the total employment threshold to 15 000 (as proposed in section 4.1). At the same time, the logical operator in step 1 of the algorithm has been altered to 'AND', along with a reduction of the density level (again as outlined earlier). Finally, the DUS population minimum has been decreased to 50 000. Figure 5 maps the DUSs produced by SMLA 8, notional Thiessen polygon boundaries providing an impression of the upper-tier grouping, of those below 95% self-containment, into metropolitan city regions.

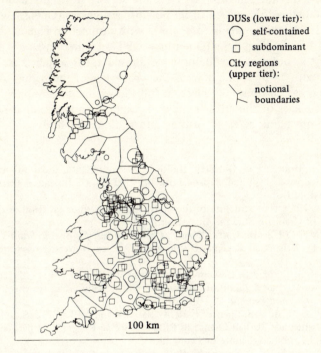

DUSs (lower tier):
○ self-contained
□ subdominant

City regions (upper tier):
⤙ notional boundaries

Figure 5. A two-tier functional regionalisation.

5 Conclusions

The work described in this paper proceeds on two basic assumptions. The first is that the concept of the daily urban system identified on the basis of journey-to-work data, of which the SMLA is an example, is theoretically sound and should in practice form the best set of areal units for the presentation of national urban data from the 1981 Census. The second assumption is that there does exist a system of functional urban areas in Britain, and that hence the task is not to try to create these entities but to find their boundaries on the basis of empirical evidence that is often inadequate for this purpose.

The conclusion of this paper is that the work so far completed tends to validate rather than undermine these assumptions. The letter and the spirit of the LSE SMLA (SMLA 1) classification both proved impossible to automate while replicating the detailed results. The positive aspect of this failure was the emphasis on the consistency inevitable from the automation of the process. There has remained a need, however, for the researchers' perceptions of the requirements of Census users and of the

geography of Britain. It can be argued that this is a necessary test for a
'good' zoning system, but by itself hardly sufficient.

It remains necessary, therefore, to evaluate the statistical indications of
any areal data units, in order to view any set of areal units within the
overall statistical framework of all possible aggregates (Openshaw and
Taylor, 1979), and perhaps compare it with optimal arrangements for
specific objective functions (Openshaw, 1977). These tasks are particularly
important in order to provide users of any data, for which these areas are
suitable, with an understanding of the properties of the zoning system.
Data analysis can then take place in full knowledge of any likely weakness
and deficiencies of the areal framework, something which, if it happens,
will be a quite unique event in the history of spatial study.

References
Berry B J L, Goheen P G, Goldstein H, 1968 "Metropolitan area definition: a re-
    evaluation of concept and statistical practice" WP-68, US Bureau of the Census,
    Washington, DC
Bogue D J, 1949 "The structure of the metropolitan community" Horace H Rackhan
    School of Graduate Studies, Ann Arbor, Mich.
Coombes M G, 1978 *Contiguity: Analysis of a Concept for Spatial Studies* DP-15,
    Centre for Urban and Regional Development Studies, University of Newcastle upon
    Tyne
Coombes M G, Dixon J S, Goddard J B, Openshaw S, Taylor P J, 1978 "Towards a
    more rational consideration of census areal units: daily urban systems in Britain"
    Environment and Planning A **10** 1179-1185
Drewett R, Goddard J B, Spence N, 1974 "SMLA's and MELA's: definitional notes
    and commentary" Urban Change in Britain Working Report 1, Department of
    Geography, London School of Economics
Drewett R, Goddard J B, Spence N, 1976 *British Cities: Urban Population and
    Employment Trends 1951-71* research report 10, Department of Employment,
    London (HMSO, London)
Hall P, Thomas R, Gracey H, Drewett R, 1973 *The Containment of Urban England*
    (George Allen and Unwin, London)
Hay D, Hall P, 1976 "Urban regionalization of Great Britain 1971" European Urban
    Systems Working Paper 1.1, Department of Geography, University of Reading,
    England
Leusmann C S, Slater P B, 1977 "A functional regionalization program based on the
    standardization and hierarchical clustering of transactions flow tables" *Computer
    Applications* **4** 769-777
Masser I, Brown P J B, 1975 "Hierarchical aggregation procedures for interaction
    data" *Environment and Planning A* **7** 509-523
Openshaw S, 1977 "A geographical solution to scale and aggregation problems in
    region-building, partitioning and spatial modelling" *Transactions of the Institute of
    British Geographers, New Series* **2** 459-472
Openshaw S, Gillard A A, 1979 "On the stability of a spatial classification of census
    enumeration data" in *London Papers in Regional Science 9. Theory and Method
    in Urban and Regional Science* Ed. P W J Batey (Pion, London) pp 178-202
Openshaw S, Taylor P J, 1979 "A million or so correlation coefficients: three
    experiments on the modifiable areal unit problem" in *Statistical Methods in the
    Spatial Sciences* Ed. N Wrigley (Pion, London) pp 127-144

Slater P B, 1976 "A hierarchical regionalization of Japanese prefectures using 1972 interprefectural migration flows" *Regional Studies* **10** 123–132

Smart M W, 1974 *Progress in Planning Volume 2, Part 4. Labour Market Areas: Uses and Definition* (Pergamon Press, Oxford)

US Bureau of the Budget, 1964 *Standard Metropolitan Statistical Areas* (US Government Printing Office, Washington, DC)

US Bureau of the Census, 1951 *Seventeenth Census of the United States: 1950* (US Government Printing Office, Washington, DC)

The Standard Metropolitan Labour Area Concept Revisited: Comment

M W SMART
Manpower Services Commission

I find that the paper by Coombes et al (this volume, pages 140–159) has some stimulating things to say, although it is tantalisingly brief in places, especially towards the end. I particularly welcome the clear exposition of the procedures by which the SMLAs have been defined and the criticisms of the difficulties and ambiguities in the way in which the procedures have been applied. As the paper says, the basis for this type of definition is a set of arbitrary rules, most of which have been imported unchanged from the US Census, and there has been a notable absence of any empirical analysis to support them. The paper is also on the ball in identifying two major weaknesses in the SMLA approach: first, the way in which contiguous areas are amalgamated; and second, the choice of employed-population thresholds. As a basis for association, contiguity does in fact prove highly ambiguous and may conceal very wide variations in the degree of interaction between areas. I think the authors are right to point to interaction as a further criterion for amalgamation, although they may well understate the changes which would result from adopting it in a consistent way. They are also right to point out the arbitrariness of the employed-population threshold adopted for SMLA definition and to indicate that more satisfactory results could be obtained by lowering it. However, the charge they make against a threshold of 20000 can also be brought against their preferred level of 15000. Given that the search for a natural threshold is, as they say, doomed to futility, is there any point in having one?

Where I should have liked to see the argument developed much further is in the last few pages. The observation in section 4.2 that "Some order seemed to exist but the available classificatory techniques, based on a priori definitional rules, seemed incapable of or inadequate for the task" seems a very fair conclusion from what has been said earlier in the paper. However, I think this points to more radical questions about possible alternatives than the authors have considered. They suggest that the results of the SMLA definition are probably the best available set of functional urban areas and are geographically sensible and intuitively right. Yet I wonder whether this judgment would be supported by a systematic examination of the various types of areas which are found useful in practice as references for policy decisions on urban problems. In at least one major area of policy—employment—the SMLAs have not in fact been found relevant and it should perhaps still be an open question whether an alternative set of areas might serve at least some policy and research needs better.

It may be that the basic presuppositions of the SMLA approach should receive closer and more critical examination than they have so far been given. There seems to me to be at least a hint of authoritarianism in the insistence on centrality as a fundamental a priori value—irrespective of whether empirical observation establishes it or not—and on associated concepts such as dominance, order, or hierarchy, suggesting a determination to impose a pattern on the data before the data have been allowed to speak for themselves. Virtually all classifications of urban regions, including the SMLAs, pay regard to commuting as a major indication of association between areas. But successive studies of commuting, from Kate Liepmann's in 1940 onwards, have shown that in most areas, including the conurbations as conventionally defined, only a minority, and often a very small minority, of work journeys are centrally oriented. The remainder are either local—the largest single component in almost every case—or follow complex cross patterns between suburbs, or else increasingly are oriented away from the centre in the reverse direction. A criterion for amalgamation of 15% commuting to the central core, such as the SMLA uses, invites the question of what the other 85% are doing and whether their work patterns should not be given equivalent weight in determining the result. For this reason, it seems more satisfactory to begin with home–workplace relationships as they actually *are*, replacing the illusive concept of *centrality* with one of *meaningful locality* which can be precisely measured by the extent to which a given area—whether urban or rural—is self-contained in labour market terms. This at least is the principle on which the travel-to-work areas used by the Department of Employment have been defined and respect for the data produces results which in some cases are strikingly different from those obtained on the basis of the SMLAs. In particular, all but one of the provincial conurbations, which all fall within unitary areas under the SMLA definition, are found to consist of two or more separate labour market areas. Locality is an important human, social and political value and a classification which ignores, for example, the objectively demonstrated separateness of Leeds and Bradford—which both had over 80% self-containment in 1971—is not going to be very useful as a reference for tackling the employment problems of either of them.

One final question is whether it is useful to work on a definition which covers only a part of the national territory and which, however far it is stretched, still leaves many awkward residual areas. The authors of the paper see difficulties in a classification which ignores the difference between Liverpool and Taunton. Yet employment—and many other— problems do not stop at the conurbation or SMLA boundary, and the measurement of unemployment—its relative severity and the extent to which it calls for remedy from a limited amount of resources which have to be deployed over the nation as a whole—is of as much concern to one area as to the other. For this reason, it is logical and right that the Department of Employment should treat Liverpool and Taunton on the same footing by publishing in the Employment Gazette unemployment percentages for the appropriate travel-to-work areas, which have been defined by applying objective and broadly consistent criteria of self-containment over the whole country.

I should have liked to see the concluding argument carried further to cover these issues. However, the discussion on two-tier functional regionalisation in section 4.3—almost the curtain line of the paper—opens up a very promising line of enquiry by considering the feasibility of a classification which would recognise, for example, both the local identity of Southport and its relationship to the wider Merseyside area. This approach acknowledges that different areas are needed for different purposes, and especially for a useful representation of labour market realities as distinct from the wider metropolitan relationships which the SMLA is trying, not so far very successfully, to combine with them.

If the approach could be developed by the study of actual work-journey patterns along with other relevant links, it could produce results more firmly grounded in experience. This would do justice both to the concept of meaningful locality and to its wider metropolitan or subregional relationships and would thus avoid the weaknesses in the SMLA concept which the authors have so sharply identified.

Previous volumes in the series

Volume 3

Volume 4

Contents of previous volumes

Volume 5

Volume 6

Volume 7

The Regional Effects of the Crisis on the Forms of Organisation of Production and Location of Industry in the Mediterranean Basin
J-P Laurençin, J-C Monateri, C Palloix, R Tiberghien, P Vernet

Regional Relations and Economic Structure in the EEC *R Lee*

Central and Peripheral Regions in a Process of Economic Development: The Italian Case
B Secchi

Coal Combines and Interregional Uneven Development in the UK
J Carney, J Lewis, R Hudson

Multinationals, Spatial Inequalities, and Workers' Control *Oonagh McDonald*

An Impact Analysis of Environmental Attraction Profiles and Spatial Mobility
P Nijkamp

Calibrating a Disaggregated Residental Allocation Model—DRAM *S H Putman*

On Hierarchical Dynamics *W Isard*

Urban Simulation—The Vancouver Experience *M Goldberg*

Spatial Externalities and Locational Conflict *M Dear*

Volume 8

Demometrics of Migration and Settlement *A Rogers*

An Alternative Model of the Central-place System *J B Parr*

The Potential of the Microbehavioural Approach to Regional Analysis *R Leigh, D J North*

Accumulation, the Regional Problem, and Nationalism *J Carney, J Lewis* (Editors)

The Politics of Epistemology in Regional Science *J Lewis, B Melville*

On the Stability of a Spatial Classification of Census Enumeration District Data
S Openshaw, A A Gillard

The Merseyside Input–Output Study and its Application in Structure Planning
J de Kanter, W I Morrison

Policy-oriented Housing Models: Some Tentative Applications
P Holm, F Snickars, J R Gustafsson, B Hårsman

Assisted Labour Mobility Policy in Britain: An Assessment of Performance
P B Beaumont

Contents of previous volumes

Volume 9

CONSTRUCTION LIBRARY,
Liverpool Polytechnic,
Victoria Street, L1 6EY

developments in urban
and regional analysis

LIVERPOOL POLYTECHNIC LIBRARY

3 1111 00125 3382

BREHENY, M.J
DEVELOPMENTS IN URBAN AND REGIONAL ANALY
MP ABE 309.262 BRE 1979

London Papers in Regional Science

p Pion Limited, 207 Brondesbury Park, London NW2 5JN